Differentiation That Really Works

Grade K–2

Strategies From Real Teachers for Real Classrooms

Differentiation That Really Works

Grade K–2

Cheryll M. Adams, Ph.D.,
and Rebecca L. Pierce, Ph.D.

PRUFROCK PRESS INC.
WACO, TEXAS

Dedication

This book is dedicated to the many teachers and students with whom we have worked in appreciation for what we have learned from them. We also dedicate this book to our families and friends for their love and support.

Prufrock Press Inc.
P.O. Box 8813
Waco, TX 76714-8813
Phone: (800) 998-2208
Fax: (800) 240-0333
http://www.prufrock.com

CONTENTS

ACKNOWLEDGEMENTS

Although there are many who write in the area of differentiation, the thoughts of Carol Tomlinson have been a tremendous influence on our work and practice. We share her passion for supporting teachers as they design learning environments that meet the needs of diverse learners. She has inspired us to seek out teachers who are practicing professionals and have embraced differentiation. The teachers we selected have or are working toward their license in gifted education. It has been our privilege to work with them, and we appreciate their willingness to share their work. We gratefully acknowledge the following teachers, whose contributions are found in this book:

Shannon Anderson
Sharon Boggs
Rhonda Brandt
Molly Davis
Christine Gesse
Allison Gill
Jaci Greig
Vicki Heil
Barbara Katenkamp

Mandy Keele
Emily Kubek
Julia Lester
Loree Marroquin
Alicia Mathis
Melinda Millholland
Erin Mohr
Maura Mundell
Ashley Peters

Debra Raines
Kimberly Sapikowski
Kristen Sell
Kristen Shively
Ali Wade
Tamara Weller
Melissa Yekulis

CHAPTER 1

INTRODUCTION

Why We Wrote This Book

Many years ago, we were classroom teachers ourselves, and we spent time working with students, trying to understand their needs. We read some of the early work of A. Harry Passow and Sandy Kaplan coming out of the National/State Leadership Training Institute of the 1970s, and thus began our journey toward learning how to differentiate instruction to meet the needs of all of the learners in our classroom. We both found early on in our teaching careers that giving all students the same assignment resulted in some students doing well while others were bored or frustrated. Thus, we learned how to differentiate as a means of surviving and allowing students to thrive. We learned that "more" and "faster" were not better for our gifted students, but that we needed qualitatively different work that centered on broad-based themes, issues, and problems. We learned that in order to achieve, all of our students required choice and challenge. Now that we have left the precollege classroom and are teaching at the university level, we still have to differentiate to meet the needs of our undergraduate and graduate students.

Currently, we work together at the Center for Gifted Studies and Talent Development on a number of projects related to differentiated instruction and meeting the needs of learners in the classroom. The Center is located in Burris Laboratory School on the campus of Ball State University. The proximity of the Center to the Laboratory School provides us the opportunity to work with teachers and students on a regular basis so we do not lose our important connection to what is actually happening in classrooms today. Working in the Laboratory School and in other schools throughout the United States, we have been able to use our practitioners' and researchers' lenses to identify strategies that work well in the classroom.

The strategies that we have chosen to include in this book had to meet several criteria: they had to (1) be easy to implement, (2) be easy to modify, (3) encourage student engagement, (4) have inherent opportunities for differentiation, and (4) be appropriate for multiple grade levels. The strategies we've selected do not make an exhaustive list of differentiation strategies, but they are the ones that we see being used most often by real teachers who differentiate well. Although there is little empirical evidence to support the use of these strategies, the practice-based evidence is widespread (Coil, 2007; Gregory & Chapman, 2002; Kingore, 2004; Tomlinson, 2003; Winebrenner, 1992). We think these strategies are vital for teachers to have in their bags of tricks if they want to provide choice and challenge for all learners in their classrooms. However, quality differentiation requires more than just a simple bag of tricks.

Working with teachers for more than 14 years nationally and internationally, we found some who were differentiating to a high degree and some who were just beginning to differentiate. We found some who did it well and some who struggled. Comparing and contrasting those teachers who differentiated well from their colleagues who struggled allowed us to zero in on classroom components that seemed to make the difference. What we found was that many teachers were using strategies to differentiate instruction, but they lacked the management to facilitate multiple groups working on different activities. Others had interesting lessons and activities, but when some students finished early, chaos ensued. Some teachers differentiated a lesson by providing several paths to reach the same goal, but all students were required to complete the same assessment. Those teachers who had the most successful classrooms not only used differentiated learning strategies, but also made use of anchoring activities, classroom management, and differentiated assessment. Realizing that these four components were necessary led to the development of our model, Creating an Integrated Response for Challenging Learners Equitably: A Model by Adams and Pierce (CIRCLE MAP; Adams & Pierce, 2006). We have realized that when teachers have all four components clearly articulated and they implement them, the stage is set for successful differentiation.

We learned something else with our teachers: Regardless of their levels of experience and the effectiveness of their differentiation, everyone's issue was time. We have had the privilege of coming in contact with teachers who differentiate in their classrooms on a daily basis. These classrooms are "pockets of excellence" where teachers embrace the differentiation mindset and look at everything they do through the differentiation lens. We felt other teachers could gain some time by using lessons that practicing professionals had already created and tested in their own classrooms. The lessons in this book can be used as written or modified to meet the needs of your own classroom. We have provided templates that can be used to develop your own materials using the strategies included here.

How Is This Book Different From Every Other Book on Differentiated Strategies?

This book is different because real teachers designed the lessons. Practicing professionals (everyday classroom teachers in the trenches) tested them in their own heterogeneous classrooms. These professionals differentiate on a regular basis. We have included comments from the teacher who developed each lesson describing how to use the strategy and how his or her students responded to the activity. In addition, for many lessons, we have included comments and reactions from other teachers who have used the strategies.

How to Use This Book

The following steps should be kept in mind as you make your way through the book:
1. Choose the strategy you want to implement.
2. Look at the sample lessons.
3. Don't be afraid to modify a lesson to fit your grade level and the needs of your own students.
4. Use the template to design your own lesson.
5. Use it in your classroom and enjoy!

CIRCLE MAP Model

What Is Differentiation?

Although its early focus denoted modifying curricula to meet the needs of the gifted and talented (Passow, 1982; Ward, 1980), differentiation has since taken center stage as a means of meeting the needs of academically diverse students in the heterogeneous classroom through modifying the curriculum and learning experiences of these students (Tomlinson, 1999, 2001, 2003). Differentiation is not a collection of strategies; it is not simply offering students choices; it is not group work. Although these options may be found in a differentiated classroom, differentiation involves finding multiple ways to structure learning so that each student has an opportunity to work at a moderately challenging level. It is an organized yet flexible way of proactively adjusting teaching and learning to meet students where they are, while helping all students achieve maximum growth as learners (Tomlinson, 1999). Put succinctly, differentiation is a mindset, a lens to use in examining every aspect of the classroom. Instruction may be differentiated in content, process, product, learning environment, and affect according to the students' readiness, interest, and learning profiles. For example, all of the students in a given class may be studying force and motion (content), but the laboratory experiments in which they participate may be at varying levels of complexity to accommodate their different stages of academic readiness for a particular task (process).

Successful differentiation will occur in the classroom when a number of essential elements are also addressed. These essential elements include specific classroom management techniques that address the special needs of a differentiated classroom through flexible use of time, space, and student groups; planned use of anchoring activities; a variety of differentiated instructional strategies; and differentiated assessment (Adams & Pierce, 2006).

The Model

Having worked with preservice and in-service teachers over the last decade to help implement differentiated instructional strategies in their classrooms, we have noticed several commonalities among teachers who are successful. As a result of this research, we developed the CIRCLE MAP model. The CIRCLE MAP, shown in Figure 1, is appropriate for any grade level and content area. It weaves together four elements—classroom management techniques, anchoring activities, differentiated instructional strategies, and differentiated assessment—that we found to be the commonalities among teachers who differentiated successfully. Having observed teachers across the country and internationally, we found these elements consistently in classrooms that addressed the needs of all students. For a complete discussion of the model, see Adams and Pierce (2006).

Our purpose in writing this book is to introduce you to a variety of strategies that may assist you in differentiating curriculum and instruction in your own classroom. We make the assumption that you have a good working knowledge of the differentiation mindset. If you don't, we encourage you to read Carol Tomlinson's work (1999, 2001, 2003) for a complete discussion of the topic.

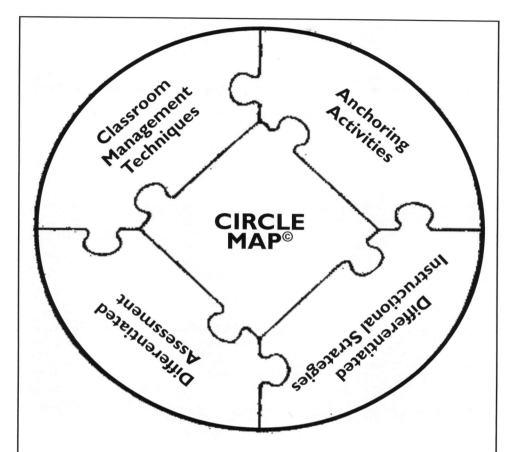

Figure 1. Creating an Integrated Response for Challenging Learners Equitably: A Model by Adams and Pierce©.

CHAPTER 2

EXIT CARDS

Overview

An exit card is a tool used by teachers to gather data about student learning. Generally, exit cards are used to gather formative data that a teacher can then use to plan the next step. The exit card is provided to students at the end of a lesson, and the teacher collects the cards as students either exit the classroom or exit one activity before going on to the next in the same classroom. Exit cards may also be known by other names, such as "ticket to leave" or "door pass." Exit cards generally have only a few questions for students to answer. Sometimes the card may ask students to respond to an overall idea that was discussed in class; at other times, students may have two or three math problems to work on that are similar to problems demonstrated in class.

How and When to Use Exit Cards

Exit cards are used at the end of a class, an activity, or a lesson. The teacher collects the completed exit cards and sorts the cards into piles based on the students' responses. There may be a group of students who clearly understand the ideas presented in the lesson and another group of students who clearly have gaps in their knowledge. There may be other students who fall between the two groups. The information from the exit cards allows the teacher to plan the next steps of instruction to address the different learning needs of the students.

Directions for Making Exit Cards

Exit cards are simple to design. For example, an exit card can be a piece of paper that the student uses to write down answers to a set of questions dictated by the teacher. Students may use their own paper, or the teacher may hand out paper from the classroom recycle box. Index cards and Post-It® Notes are also simple and easy to use as exit cards, although somewhat more expensive. Some teachers may wish to customize their exit cards for a specific lesson or activity.

How This Strategy Fits in the CIRCLE MAP

Exit cards are an important data-gathering tool for formative assessment in the differentiated classroom. As such, they are essential to the "differentiated assessment" component of the CIRCLE MAP.

Examples

The examples we have chosen include exit cards that can be readily adapted to many topics. These cards were created by real teachers who have used them in their own classrooms. Where possible, we have included comments from both the teachers and their colleagues, with the intention that the comments may provide additional insight into using the exit card for another topic.

For example, Brooke Brown is a kindergarten teacher who has decided to implement exit cards in her class this year. She creates a card to help her determine who can recognize the letter "K." She wants to be sure that all her students are able to understand her directions and can respond appropriately. She designs a simple card with four letters in outline form: A, F, K, and R. She gives all of the children cards and directs them to color the letter K. Students write their names or initials on the cards. Students work with file folders around their papers to eliminate their ability to see what other students are doing. As Ms. Brown collects the cards, she can easily determine who can recognize the letter K by noting which letter is colored. This will allow her to determine the entry point for each child in the next lesson.

Name:_____ Date:_____

Template

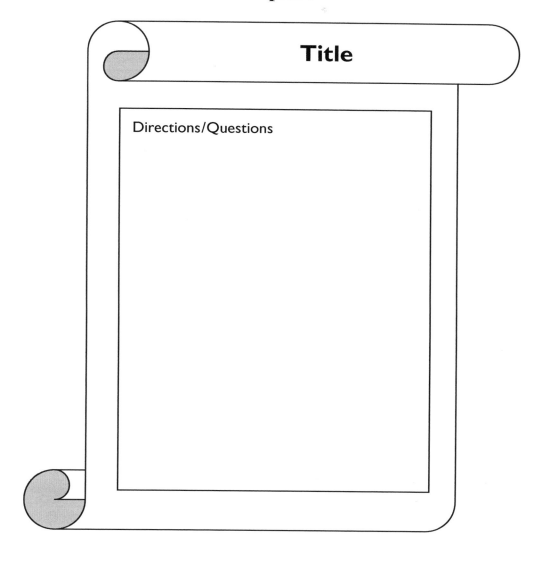

Title

Directions/Questions

Name:_____ Date:_____

Short Vowel
Exit Card

1. Write the word that tells me what the picture above is.

2. Which letter in that word makes the short vowel sound?

3. Write at least two more words that have the same short vowel sound.

Created by Alicia Mathis

Real Teacher Comments

I was a little worried about using exit cards with my kindergarten students at first. I started on my first one and realized how easy and useful it would be. I passed out sheets of decorated paper that I have been saving for no reason at all (maybe to collect dust). I read the exit cards to the students. I was surprised at how well they responded to the task without telling each other the answer. When looking at the results, they were easy to sort according to who knew what information. I based my first sort on the word. I was able to get three piles easily. Almost everyone got the vowel, so I knew that with a couple of individual conferences, I could move on. Finally, the additional words gave me a good idea of who knew the vowel sound or not.

Using the exit cards was a much easier alternative than asking the same questions 21 times. I will definitely incorporate them into the classroom more often.

—Alicia Mathis (Teacher)

What a great tool for conferencing with parents. They are quick and very easy to understand. They show parents exactly if their child knows the information or not.

—Christina (Colleague)

Name:_____ Date:_____

Exit Card

Draw three things that begin with the letter sound: A

Write one new word you learned that starts with the letter sound: A

Created by Melissa Yekulis

Real Teacher Comments

I teach kindergarten, where one of the biggest focuses of the curriculum is phonetics. The exit card was used to see if students were able to distinguish beginning letter sounds in a word. Children were introduced to many different words beginning with that letter throughout the day with morning message, letter bags, etc. The second section, used for identifying a word, was more informational for me about the spelling abilities of the children as they acquire new sounds. Children were not judged for not knowing how to spell a word.

—Melissa Yekulis (Teacher)

Your exit card seems very appropriate for your grade level. After using this, you will certainly be able to determine if they understand the concept or not.

—Heather (Colleague)

Exit Card

Circle the words that rhyme:

A Fox Has Caught the Chickens
   By Jack Prelutsky

A fox has caught the chickens,
But the chickens fixed the fox.
That fox is skipping dinner,
They gave him chicken pox.

Write three words that rhyme with Pop:

1.

2.

3.

Created by Kristen Sell

Real Teacher Comments

I tried the exit card in just my first-grade class. It worked amazingly well. The students loved the chance to give me feedback. I will definitely try it for all of my other classes in the coming weeks; I'm interested to see the feedback from the higher grade levels!

—Kristen Sell (Teacher)

What a nice exit card. I think you will find out who knows rhyming words and who doesn't.

—Alicia (Colleague)

Name:_____ Date:_____

Exit Card

Write one thing you learned today in social studies.	Write one question you still have about goods and services.
Draw a picture of a community worker who provides a service.	How would you explain the difference between a good and a service to another student?

Created by Maura Mundell

Real Teacher Comments

I presented my exit card on goods and services to my second grade class. We have been working on a unit about community helpers and goods and services for a couple of weeks. After looking at the exit cards, the students really seem to know the difference between goods and services! The last box where I asked them to explain the difference gave a few students a hard time, but then I had them answer orally, and they could explain it. I may just have to work on getting those thoughts on paper.

—Maura Mundell (Teacher)

I like that you cover different strategies in your exit card. You start very broad, asking the students what they learned in social studies, and then you specifically talk about goods and services. You have them writing both statements and questions. The second row of questions (bottom two boxes) are great because they require the students to apply their knowledge in order to compare and contrast as well as draw a community worker. Great job!

—Erin (Colleague)

I like the variety to your card—the students get to draw as well as write. I agree with the written explanation parts being difficult.

—Sharon (Colleague)

I like that you had the students draw a picture; that's very good for the visual learners or for the students who still struggle with writing. I think I might use that in a future exit card as well.

—Kimberly (Colleague)

Sharks Exit Card

Tell one way that a shark is different from most fish.

Tell something that you learned about shark teeth.

Tell something interesting and new that you learned about sharks.

Created by Julia Lester

Real Teacher Comments

I used the exit cards with my second-grade literacy group. The group consists of nine students who are reading above grade level. This week we started a new book, *Sharks*. There are seven chapters in the book. After reading the first three chapters, I wanted to assess student learning before moving forward in the book. This is a Reading A-Z book, so the chapters are just a couple of pages long. We had read Introduction, Physical Characteristics, and Eating. I included three prompts:

- Tell one way a shark is different from most fish.
- Tell something that you learned about shark teeth.
- Tell something interesting and new that you learned about sharks.

I clarified to the students that I wanted something they had learned from the book. A few had told me information they had learned from other sources earlier, when I introduced the book, but I wanted to know what they had comprehended from the reading.

All of the students could tell me something about shark teeth and something new they had learned. I found through this, though, that several were confused about sharks and fish. They knew that sharks are fish, but they believed that only sharks eat other fish, and that sharks are the largest fish. We were able to go back and read this again and discuss the fact that some other fish also eat fish.

The exit card was very beneficial to me and my students. I was able to quickly design one and assess student understanding. I will use exit cards again at the end of the shark book to assess student understanding. It was wonderful to be able to give students immediate feedback. I am already thinking of other ways to use the exit cards with my other students.

—Julia Lester (Teacher)

I am really interested in how to differentiate instruction with younger elementary students. I have found that even though some of the gifted students have superior ranges of abilities, their interests cover a full spectrum that actually includes some primary topics. I especially like the last prompt, which allows the kids to tell you what they learned. This is always interesting because it can sometimes be the most random fact that the kids are drawn toward. It was also interesting to discover where they had fallen short so you could revisit the topic.

—Jennifer (Colleague)

Name:_____ Date:_____

"I am a paleontologist."

Name one type of fossil that we talked about and describe an example.

When you classify objects, what are you doing?

Write one question that you still have after our discussion.

Created by Mandy Keele

Real Teacher Comments

I had a lesson planned this week on classification—tied to fossils. They Might Be Giants has a great new science CD/DVD out with a song called "I Am a Paleontologist." We listened to it first while following along with the lyrics on our SmartBoard. Then we brainstormed what we thought a paleontologist might do and what types of tools he or she might use to do his or her job, and we eventually discussed the four different types of fossils, analyzing examples of each. I had several bags of shark teeth, so the children were put into groups to classify them. As a group, they were to decide which characteristics they would use for their sorting criteria. Next, they made trace fossils using play-doh and either a shell or a plastic dinosaur.

After we'd finished the lesson, I handed out my exit cards. After reviewing the children's responses, I was able to sort them into three groups. I was most interested in whether or not they grasped the concept of classification. There were seven children who wrote about classification being similar to sorting based on what things looked like. We had talked about characteristics, and I did have one child attempt to spell that word. There were nine children who were able to describe a type of fossil, and maybe they mentioned something about classifying the shark teeth . . . but they didn't fully explain the concept. Then there were six children who didn't fully grasp it.

Overall, I was so excited with how well the exit cards worked. They didn't take long to create or administer, and the additional questions the children came up with were wonderful. It was a great quick assessment that was able to let me know which children needed some additional instruction.

—Mandy Keele (Teacher)

Seeing your card makes me curious about what types of questions the students came up with, too. Also, I wanted to say that my junior kindergarten class and I studied archaeologists last summer, just briefly, and we also made play-doh fossils with shells and dinosaurs. They loved it! We also have these giant "water" tubs in our room that we fill, and I filled one with sand and dinosaurs and shells and such. Then I gave the students science goggles, shovels, sand sifting tools, gloves, etc., and they had a riot. They pretended they were in a fossil dig. It was so much fun, and I felt they got to really experience the idea of paleontology and archeology.

—Kimberly (Colleague)

Name:_____ Date:_____

Fact Family

In the space below, please show me the four (4) related facts for the numbers 5, 4, and 9.

Created by Sharon Boggs

Real Teacher Comments

I used my exit card as we wrapped up a math unit on fact families. I liked how quick and simple it was to use. I now know which students have a firm grasp of this concept and which students still need some reinforcement. One additional comment I would like to add about my exit card is that I was able to see which format of addition and subtraction (vertical or horizontal) the students were comfortable with. The majority gave me answers in the horizontal format.

—Sharon Boggs (Teacher)

Great point! The open-endedness of this exit card really allows you to see how students are most comfortable organizing their work. I like that! It's really important to see how students think.

—Cindy (Colleague)

AMELIA BEDELIA EXIT CARD

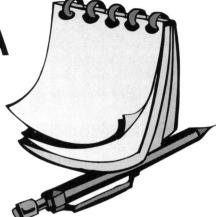

1. What are two funny things Amelia did on her first day at work?

2. In your opinion, why didn't Amelia get fired?

3. Describe Amelia using three of your favorite words.

Created by Christine Gesse

Real Teacher Comments

I used the exit card in a second-grade classroom after reading *Amelia Bedelia* with the students. Question 1's answers were varied and predictable. Question 2's answers really surprised me with much deeper thinking and reasoning than I had expected from some of the kids. Question 3 was really interesting because I told kids they could not use words like cool and awesome. I was looking for signs of creativity and got answers like nonworldly, different, and diverse. I can't wait to get back in this class and teach them about idioms in the book.

—Christine Gesse (Teacher)

I loved your card, and I could see how your students could be drawn into the activity and excited about giving their ideas. Your questions would really elicit some wonderful responses that would get them using their brains, I think. It looks like not only a fun activity, but also a very informative one about the students' thinking.

—Ashley (Colleague)

I loved the *Amelia Bedelia* books when I was younger. In my classroom, I have a set of the Scholastic *Dictionary of Idioms*—a great resource! I had students write a dialogue between two people one time, and they could only speak with idioms. It knocked their socks off!

—Sam (Colleague)

Exit Card

What was the main topic covered in today's math lesson? Name one term and its definition that was discussed today.	Order these fractions from least to greatest using a number line on the back of this paper. ¼, ⅛, 1/12, ½, ⅙, 1/9, 1/11, ⅓, 1/7, 1/10, ⅕
If you could ask me to reteach one portion of this lesson, what would it be? (What didn't you understand?)	If you did not understand a part of today's lesson, what are you going to do to help yourself learn what was taught? (Will you ask peers, a teacher, or a parent?)

Created by Melinda Millholland

Real Teacher Comments

I used this exit card with my class and discovered it is better to have only one prompt in the first box. Students only answered one prompt, because both were detailed. In the second box, I had them demonstrate knowledge of the topic we discussed in class. I think this could have been a card of its own. The third box was important because it told me what they did not understand about the lesson. I had some kids ask me what they should do if they understood everything. I asked them to tell me what they wanted to learn more about. I might add that to the box. The last box helped me remind them that they are responsible for their own learning. I had various responses, and most said they would ask me.

—Melinda Millholland (Teacher)

This card is a valuable tool, because I bet it only took 5 minutes to administer and 5 more minutes to assess understanding. That gets at a lot of data in only a few minutes!

—Jenny (Colleague)

Doubles + 1 Facts

Solve: 5 + 6 = _____

Put the steps in order:

_____ Add 1

_____ Find the smaller number

_____ Double it

Write another doubles + 1 fact:

[ ]

One other thing I learned is: _____

_____

_____

Created by Kristen Shively

Real Teacher Comments

My first graders are currently working on strategies used to solve addition facts. My exit card is very skill-based, focusing on if the students can identify one of the "Doubles + 1" facts we have been working on, on one of the strategies they can use to solve it, and on making up one of their own facts. My students liked how short it was—plus, first graders love anything you call a "ticket"! I used the term "Ticket to Leave for Music Class" rather than "Exit Card," and they were excited to complete it.

—Kristen Shively (Teacher)

What a great way to double-check your students' progress in understanding.

—Sara (Colleague)

CHAPTER 3

CHOICE BOARDS

Overview

A choice board, sometimes called a Tic-Tac-Toe board, is a tool to provide students with choice and challenge. It has nine squares arranged in a three by three grid. Directions are placed in each square. Students choose three squares to complete a winning tic-tac-toe: three in a row, three in a column, or three diagonally. The directions may be for a product or for extended practice. Choices can provide enrichment, acceleration, or additional practice, depending on how the choice board is designed. Generally, students are producing three products that provide formative or summative data for the teacher.

How and When to Use Choice Boards

Choice boards can be used at the beginning or the end of a unit, or anywhere in between. The length of time students have to complete their three choices varies with the teacher's purpose. Some choice boards are designed to be completed in a week (e.g., one that deals with weekly spelling words). Other times, a choice board may last for longer periods of time, depending on the complexity of the choices or the length of time the teacher chooses for activities to be completed. Choice boards may be tiered to accommodate varying learning needs when a wider range of choice and challenge is needed. The completed activities from the choice board can be used by the teacher to plan the next steps of instruction, to assess students' progress or level of understanding, or to help with assigning grades.

Directions for Making Choice Boards

Choice boards are simple to design using the template provided here. The table function in a word processing program is another easy way to create choice boards. Each cell contains directions for or a description of an activity to be completed. Once the activities are appropriately sequenced—so that no matter how the student chooses to make tic-tac-toe, there is variety—the choice board can be printed and copied. We have found that putting the activities on Post-It® Notes allows for experimentation with multiple arrangements until the "best" placement is found. Then we use a word processing program to produce the final form of the choice board for students. Choose the way that works best with your particular style of creating classroom materials. Keep in mind that some activities will require rubrics, while others may be self-checking, and students will need to know where to find answer keys.

How This Strategy Fits in the CIRCLE MAP

Choice boards fit in the "differentiated instructional strategies" component of the CIRCLE MAP. They provide a simple yet lively means of varying the process or product in a differentiated classroom.

Examples

The examples we have chosen to include here address specific topics. These choice boards were created by real teachers who have used them in their own classrooms. When possible, we have included comments, both from those teachers and from their colleagues, with the intention that they may provide additional insight into creating your own choice board. We have tried to include a wide variety of topics to give you a number of ideas for making your own.

For example, in Jason Williams' second-grade classroom, students are busily working on a choice board he has designed as part of his science unit on weather. In each of the nine blocks, he has placed an interesting activity to reinforce or enrich the concepts he has chosen. He taught the students how to play tic-tac-toe before introducing the choice board so that they would understand how to make their choices of activities. Mr. Williams has been careful to include activities that will appeal to various strengths and learning profiles. He has developed some activities that encourage movement and some that are more analytic. Some activities require research, and some rely on reinforcing facts. By providing activities of varying readiness levels, and by addressing different learning profiles, he is ensuring that all of his students will find challenging and meaningful activities to complete.

Name:_____ Date:_____

Template
Title of Choice Board

Directions: Please select three assignments to complete for a winning tic-tac-toe (3 in the same row, 3 in the same column, or 3 diagonally).

Differentiation That Really Works (Grades K–2) © Prufrock Press Inc. • Permission is granted to photocopy or reproduce this page for classroom use only.

Name:_____ Date:_____

Tic-Tac-Toe

Directions: Choose three activities to do. Your three choices must be three in a row and make a tic-tac-toe!

Story: "Jan's New Home"
Comprehension Skill: Sequencing

Interpersonal	Musical	Verbal-Linguistic
How do you think Jan felt at the beginning, middle, and end of the story? Write about it in your journal.	Design a song or a rap to perform that retells what happens in "Jan's New Home."	Use the story-telling cards to retell the story to a partner. Mix up the cards and see if your partner can put them in order.
Visual-Spatial Design a postcard for Jan to send to her friends at her old school. Your picture should include things from her new home.	**Reread "Jan's New Home."** You may • read by yourself, • read with a partner, or • listen to the story. You must do this!	**Intrapersonal** Jan might have kept a journal during her move. Write one journal entry that Jan may have written at the beginning of her move and one at the end.
Logical-Mathematical Make a timeline about Jan's move. What did she see? What did she do?	**Naturalist** Jan sees a city and a farm on her trip. Complete a Venn diagram. List things she sees in these places.	**Bodily-Kinesthetic**  Use the puppets to act out the beginning, middle, or end of "Jan's New Home." Write down what the characters say to each other.

Created by Kristen Shively

Real Teacher Comments

I chose to make my choice board revolve around the comprehension skill of sequencing to go along with a story in our reading basal. I tried to design one activity that would appeal to each of Gardner's multiple intelligences. (The copy my students got did not have the intelligence listed on it—this copy does.) I chose to try this out with my higher level first-grade students, because I thought some of the directions were a little complex for some of my middle and lower level readers, and they are still really concentrating on decoding while reading, not as much on comprehension. My higher level students were up to the challenge. From the talk about ideas and excitement I heard, their products will hopefully be high quality!

—Kristen Shively (Teacher)

I loved your choice board. We have the same basal series, and we also did the story "Jan's New Home" last week. I hope it is OK with you that I save this file and use it next year. I loved your graphics, and I liked the variety of activities that you provided.

—Sharon (Colleague)

This is great! I love the idea of relating each square to a different Gardner intelligence. The graphics are very cool and add to the interest. I think the questions are thought provoking and challenging, but appropriate for first graders. I can see why they were excited!

—Kristen E. (Colleague)

I also plan to "borrow" your choice board. I love the use of MI. This is a perfect story for which to make a choice board; it's one the kids like to read. The graphics added the special touch. Thanks!

—Christine (Colleague)

Solar System Tic-Tac-Toe

This tic-tac-toe is for a first-grade science self-contained high-ability classroom. The Indiana standards covered include 1.1.1, 1.1.2, 1.2.6, 1.3.3, 1.3.4, 1.3.5, and 1.5.2. Students would need to complete any three activities in a row.

Draw and label the phases of the moon.	Read the book *Stars* and write five things you learned from it about stars.	Write a song or poem about a planet and read/sing it to the class. (Turn in a copy of the words.)
List the planets in their order from the sun. Then list the planets in ABC order.	Make a Venn diagram and compare and contrast the sun and the moon, or pick any two planets to compare and contrast.	Make a chart that lists each planet. Include at least 3 categories of information for each planet. (For example, size, gravity, and atmosphere)
Make an ABC book of knowledge about the solar system.	Draw and label the planets and the sun in the solar system.	Role-play for the class as if you were a tour guide on a space shuttle, and talk briefly about each planet as you pass it by. (Turn in your script.)

Created by Shannon Anderson

Real Teacher Comments

This tic-tac-toe is similar to one I did with my first-grade class last year. My class was a general education class last year, and this year is a high-ability classroom, so I definitely kicked it up a notch. This was done during our study of the solar system in science. The standards covered are listed on the tic-tac-toe itself. I just started using these boards last year, and they were a huge hit with the kids!

—Shannon Anderson (Teacher)

Great job giving students the opportunity to complete a project from the opinion of someone other than themselves! (Act as a tour guide . . .) Several exemplary curricula underscore the importance of this opportunity for high-ability students.

—Kristen (Colleague)

I am amazed at what first graders are capable of doing! Very neat projects. I'm sure the kids love to create the projects.

—Brenda (Colleague)

I think it was a very good idea to center this directly around the content standards. It looks like fun!

—Heather (Colleague)

I really enjoyed the idea of bringing music into the lesson. I think that is a great idea—plus, it showcases multiple intelligences.

—Jason (Colleague)

I will be teaching the solar system again this school year. This gives me ideas I can adapt for fourth grade and will definitely help me get started.

—Megan (Colleague)

ABCDEFGHIJKLMN

Spelling Choice Board

DIRECTIONS:
Choose three activities to make a tic-tac-toe. Complete these in your Spelling Journal.

Sort your words into columns according to their short vowel sounds. Sort words that do not fit into any groups under the "weirdo" column. Example: <u>Short a</u> <u>Short i</u> <u>Weirdo</u> bag dig I	Clap out the syllables for your words. Write how many syllables each word has. Example: picnic = 2 can = 1	Make rhyming words for each of your spelling words. Make sure that each rhyming word is different. Example: can - man

Divide your words into syllables.
 	
Example: picnic = pic/nic
	Write a short story using all of the words from your spelling list.	Write your words in alphabetical (ABC) order.
		
		Example: bag
		          can
		          dig

Look up each word in the dictionary and write one example sentence for the definition given.	Form as many of your words into plurals as you can. Plural means more than one. Some words will not have a plural form. Example: bag-bags	Write seven sentences using as many of your words as possible. Your sentences must make sense.

abcdefghijklmnopqrstuvwxyz

Created by Emily Kubek

Real Teacher Comments

This choice board is for my second-grade students. Several of my students really liked the choice boards. I introduced what each square was, and several students started right away on activities that sounded appealing to them. What was interesting was that some students did not look at all of the activities in their tic-tac-toe all of the way through. For example, some students started on the rhyming words, and then went down to writing words in ABC order, but then they groaned when they got to writing sentences at the end. They asked me if they had to do the last one because it was not as fun or easy for them as the other two squares had been. Some of them liked the ideas, but they asked me if it was OK if they asked me questions about certain ones later, because they did not think that they would remember what it was that they were supposed to do. I explained, of course, that I would help them when they needed it!

—Emily Kubek (Teacher)

I've had students work on choice boards for spelling. They really liked working with them. After a while they remember what they are to do for the different choices. There are sites and books to give you ideas that will give a variety of choices during the year.

—Loretta (Colleague)

The tic-tac-toe board makes spelling less rote and boring! I find it very interesting how similar and yet different our activities were. I do like the dictionary activity. I also liked your graphics and examples to guide students.

—Christina (Colleague)

That's a cute choice board. I may try to do something similar with my gifted kindergarten class for my writing/reading center or when we're doing differentiated groups. I like that it's adaptable for word families, sight words, spelling words, etc. I got a kick out of the "weirdo" column. Don't our little ones love it when we use terms like that?

—Sandra (Colleague)

Beginning Math Skills

Match the number of manipulatives to the number card.	Guess how many cubes it will take to measure each object.	Fill in a pattern block picture that is already made for you.
Measure and compare your and your friends' shoestrings.	Create a design using pattern blocks. See if your friend can copy your design.	Count the items in each cup and decide which has the most.
Use your pattern blocks to complete the AB, ABB, and ABC patterns.	Create a number puzzle for your friends using stickers.	Make a picture to show how our friends are different sizes.

Created by Alicia Mathis

Real Teacher Comments

I really did not think creating the choice board was very difficult. On the other hand, implementing it was another story. My kindergarten students are still getting used to how school operates and need a lot of direction. I decided to use this choice board during a center time using my assistant. My usual center time is pretty structured, so allowing a choice was a little hectic. I can't say that I will throw this out the door, but it will take time and patience.

—Alicia Mathis (Teacher)

I can't say that I can offer any advice on implementing the choice board at the kindergarten level—I've taught third, fourth, and sixth grades. But if it makes you feel better, my sixth graders still had difficulty figuring out the possible choices! That surprised me.

I like how you used the shapes on your choice board. I'm sure that did help your kindergarten students with their choices, since they could say, "I need to do a circle . . ."

—Jessica (Colleague)

I too had a few problems with structure with my students using the choice boards. Mine were used as homework, but there were lots of questions and need for clarification. I think that if there were a rubric (especially in the older grades, when they are worried about their points), that would help guide their work. I also think that like with any new experience, it will just take time to get used to the activity. My class is also very structured, since we have very little time and lots of things to cover. My students told me that after they get the hang of it and do a few of the choice boards, it will be easier and more fun. I think that there can still be structure to activities like this, and even differentiation. If you have students who need to do the lower processing items, you can tell them the best choice for a tic-tac-toe for their ability/needs, but still allow them to choose a different one. You could have similar modifications for the higher abilities.

—Nichole (Colleague)

Alicia, I liked how you used the shapes for math choices. By the end of second semester, they will be old pros at this after they have learned some reading skills.

—Roberta (Colleague)

I like how you did your choice board at center time with direction. That probably helped lessen your students' confusion. We as teachers, myself included, tend to think of our last year students from second semester on and forget how they were first semester (still "untrained"). I'm sure that by next semester, your students will be able to do this activity with more success and less frustration on the teacher's part!

—Christina (Colleague)

I love your kindergarten choice board! I used to teach kindergarten, and something like this would have been great for some of my center activities, or independent work, or even during some of those days where we had inside recess. I like how all of your activities are hands-on, too.

—Emily (Colleague)

Name:_____ Date:_____

Second-Grade Spelling Choice Board

Students will have three items that they must pick from the tic-tac-toe board (one 10-point item and two 5-point items). This contract will be given to the student every Monday and must be signed by a parent and turned in on Friday. This contract will count toward your child's spelling grade. It is worth up to 20 points. Students may work on this at home or at school. They may choose to do columns or diagonals, but not rows.

List of words:

read	feel	easy	deep	seats
party	wheel	leave	windy	sleep
teeth	team	murmur	clenched	stagnant
defrauding	cautioned	reprovingly	sacrifice	hesitate

Sentence: The students were cautioned not to leave their seats.

Create a comic strip using at least 10 words. ____/10 pts	Find an antonym or a synonym for each spelling word. ____/10 pts	Cut the letters/words out of a newspaper or magazine to form each word. ____/10 pts
Use shape boxes to form each word. **Example: g i r a f f e** ____/5 pts	Write a sentence for each word. ____/5 pts	Write your words in pen and circle all of the vowels. ____/5 pts
Solve the word search on the back of this contract. ____/5 pts	Divide each word into syllables. ____/5 pts	Scramble each word and find a friend or family member to unscramble them. ____/5 pts

Staple all work to the back of this contract, sign here, and return by Friday.

Student Signature _____

Parent Signature _____

Created by Melinda Millholland

Real Teacher Comments

This is the Spelling Choice Board format that I use each week. They have time to work on it in class as well as at home. Students enjoy working on their choice of assignments. Because it does lend itself to many different types of activities, I have very few students who do not turn in their boards. This is an awesome way for students to choose their own learning activities.

—Melinda Millholland (Teacher)

These activities sound like a lot of fun and help the students learn the material in a unique way. I also like how you involve the parent.

—Marlon (Colleague)

Melinda, this is a great way to encourage self-learning and self-management of time and materials. It also shows respect for the students, because you state specifically that they may work on it either at home or at school—another choice for them to make!

—Sherri (Colleague)

Melinda, I loved this board. I am going to use some of these general ideas to improve my instruction with my college math students—obviously, not the same tasks, but I see ideas I can glean to incorporate into my instructional plans.

—Julie (Colleague)

I really like your board and the point values. I can see how it allows the students flexibility, and they know what they are getting as far as a grade if they do a good job.

—Lori (Colleague)

Name:_____ Date:_____

Charlotte's Web
Choice Board: Choose Three
Activities to Make Tic-Tac-Toe

It's carnival time!

You are in charge of organizing the carnival for your town.
1. List six different rides you will have at your carnival. (Be creative when naming the rides.)
2. Plan, set, and explain pricing for your carnival.
3. Create a poster to be used at your carnival that lists prices, deals, and rides.

Compare/contrast

Use a Venn diagram to compare/contrast two of the characters from the story. You must have at least four elements in each section.

Persuasive writing

In the story, Uncle receives the blue ribbon. You have two choices. Choose either Number 1 or Number 2.
1. Argue why Wilbur should have gotten the blue ribbon. Give at least two good reasons.
2. Defend the choice that Uncle deserved the blue ribbon. Give at least two good reasons.

3-D fun

Design your very own diorama. Create a setting for the farm animals.

Pig poetry

Create a poem about Wilbur. Make your poem an Ode. (Use poetry resources provided in classroom for additional help.)

Creepy crawly!

Use the resources in the spider tub to find out more about the anatomy of the spider. Then, create a diagram showing the anatomy of a spider. Be sure to label the diagram. You may use any resource you like to create your diagram.

"Old MacDonald Had a Farm" "The Itsy-Bitsy Spider"

Both songs mentioned above are great, fun songs. Create your own farm or farm animal song. Be prepared to help the class learn the song.

Itsy-bitsy spider!

Use the information provided in the classroom to create a graph about four different types of spiders. Pick one of the types of spiders and write an informational paragraph about it.

Down on the farm

Much of the story takes place on a farm. Create a board game that has characters from the story and deals with the events of and items found on a farm.

Created by Vicki Heil

Real Teacher Comments

I used a *Charlotte's Web* tic-tac-toe last year when we read the book. However, after learning about high-ability students, I totally tweaked it. The students were given a certain amount of time each day to work during the week and were also allowed to work on their boards during any extra time they had. They were allowed to gather materials and information outside of class if needed. The students enjoyed the power of being able to choose which three boxes they wanted to do. After we were finished, I asked for feedback from the students. Many said it was a welcome change of pace, that they had found out a little bit about themselves in regard to which types of activities they'd picked, that they'd loved seeing everyone's unique take on the assignments, and that it didn't feel like work.

—Vicki Heil (Teacher)

This is my favorite book, so sometimes I wish that I could teach it just for that reason. I appreciated the very creative choices there for those students of high ability musically and creatively.

—Erin (Colleague)

I love *Charlotte's Web*. I was thinking of how I could use the concepts of friendship and conflict to develop a unit on this book. I see the amount of time needed to complete each block, and I enjoyed hearing the reactions of your students after completing the board.

—Sharon (Colleague)

I love the question that asks the students to defend Uncle's getting the Blue Ribbon or to argue why Wilbur deserved the ribbon. This helps the students with some higher levels of thinking when they have to defend their own sides of an issue.

—April (Colleague)

Name:_____ Date:_____

I have a dream...

Choice Board—Freedom

Choose an activity from each column.

1	2	3
Read *Coretta Scott King* by Teri Crawford Jones and take the Accelerated Reader quiz.	Explain what segregation is and give at least one example.	With two other people, reenact Rosa Parks' bus experience. (One person is Rosa, one person is the bus driver, and one is the person for whom Rosa would not give up her seat.)
Watch the Martin Luther King, Jr. biography on http://www.brainpopjr.com. Take the online quiz and print your score.	In his "I Have a Dream" speech, Martin Luther King, Jr. uses repetition. Write your own speech using repetitive phrases.	Create a timeline of important events in Martin Luther King, Jr.'s life (this can be with pictures, words, or both).
Read *The Other Side* by Jacqueline Woodson and fill out a compare/contrast chart for the main characters.	Write at least three questions that you would like to ask Martin Luther King, Jr. if he were alive today.	Choose a rule you must follow either at home or at school and create an oral argument for why you think that rule should be changed.

Created by Mandy Keele

Real Teacher Comments

Prior to using this choice board, I've always used tic-tac-toe boards as a culminating activity. Over the last week, we've been talking about freedom and segregation. I liked calling it a choice board because the students were all very excited and loved getting to select their choices. The children enjoyed it, and their products were, for the most part, well executed.

I'm always so amazed at the things first graders will come up with. With the interview questions, I had several children want to ask MLK, "Why were you killed?" I turned that question back to the class. After several answers, one child said, "I think he was killed not so much because he [James Earl Ray] didn't like Martin Luther King, Jr., but because he didn't like his ideas." That spurred yet another great discussion about what we should do when we don't agree with someone else. Based on the children who picked the oral argument choice, I think I might have a couple of future lawyers. One little boy gave a stellar argument on why he should be allowed to chew gum at school.

—Mandy Keele (Teacher)

Wow! That goes right along with what my first grade literacy group is reading this week. I chose a Learning A-Z book about Rosa Parks. This has led to a discussion about MLK and segregation. I really liked your activity choices.

—Julia (Colleague)

I really liked the option to use the computer. I think it is important to have students comfortable with the computer and Internet. It's never too early to show them what a great tool/resource the computer can be!

—Jennifer (Colleague)

I was very impressed with your choice board. You used different thinking skills and a variety of products. I can see the appeal for all of the students in your classroom; you have included different interest areas.

—Jeri (Colleague)

I really liked the online activity. My students love anything they can do with computers. I also liked the reenactment activity. I think when you have students work together, it keeps them focused and accountable. I could easily adapt this to my classroom

—Maura (Colleague)

Name:_____ Date:_____

Community Workers

Directions: You must select activities in three separate boxes to make a tic-tac-toe. They can be across, up and down, or diagonal. Staple all work to this cover sheet.

List two examples of goods and two examples of services using a flipbook.	Explain the difference between a good and a service in a friendly letter to your friend.	Interview another student to learn about what he or she wants to be when he or she gets older and how that job provides a good or a service. Come up with at least five questions related to that job.
Using a brochure, organize a list of goods and services that a business of your choice would provide.	Compare and contrast two businesses that provide goods and services using a Venn diagram.	Examine four community workers who provide goods and/or services using trading cards. Each card should have a colored picture on the front and at least three facts on the back.
Create an advertisement for a local business that shares its weekly specials being offered.	Develop a word search of at least 20 words relevant to learning about community workers.	Recommend a specific job in the community by making a mobile that has at least four hanging pieces of related information about that job.

Created by Maura Mundell

Differentiation That Really Works (Grades K–2) © Prufrock Press Inc. • Permission is granted to photocopy or reproduce this page for classroom use only.

Real Teacher Comments

My choice board is a continuation of the community helper/goods and services theme we have been working on. We use choice boards often in my classroom, so this activity went well. Students were engaged and were even more creative with their choices than was asked of them. I allowed them to change things slightly, depending on how they connected their choices to our overall theme. One of my twice-exceptional students made a flipbook with *Star Wars* as his focus, and when I asked him how it tied back to goods and services, he stated that *Star Wars* is a good that provides entertainment. He was still able to make the connection while bringing in something that he was interested in. It was a pleasure to see such enthusiasm from all of my students! I had a parent in the classroom while they were working on their choice boards, and the parent made more than one comment about how great it was and how creative their products were!

—Maura Mundell (Teacher)

I have someone from our 4-H extension office visiting my classroom in February to discuss goods and services. You have some great activities that we could use to expand upon her visit.

—Mandy (Colleague)

Name:_____ Date:_____

Tic-Tac-Toe
With Books by Author
Kevin Henkes

Directions: Choose activities in a tic-tac-toe design. When you have completed the activities in a row—horizontally, vertically, or diagonally—you may decide to be finished. You may also decide to keep going and complete more activities.

I choose activities # _____, # _____, # _____, and # _____.

1. Complete a story chart on one of the books we read this week.	2. Write a story about what would have happened with the mean boys on the bike if Lilly had not been brave and chased them off. 	3. Draw a picture of your favorite character from any of the books we read this week.
4. Make a prediction and draw a picture about what would have happened if Wemberly had not met Jewel on the first day of school.	5. Take a piece of large white construction paper. Draw a character on one half and a self-portrait on the other half. In the middle, list the ways that you are the same.	6. Get with three friends. Act out a character and see if they can guess who you are.
7. Write a letter to one of the characters in our books. Introduce yourself to the character and ask him or her three questions.	8. Sort the character pictures any way you choose, but you must be able to explain your reasons for your different categories.	9. Write a story about what would have happened if Louise did not follow Sheila Ray when she went a new way home.

Created by Ali Wade

Real Teacher Comments

After our author study on Kevin Henkes, I passed out the choice board. My first graders really loved the freedom of the board. They had a hard time understanding at first that they did not have to do all nine activities. I also had to review the game of tic-tac-toe; some didn't know that they had to make a straight line. Overall it was a very fun learning project for my students.

—Ali Wade (Teacher)

I like how you used the choice board as part of an author study. This seemed to give the students a lot of choice because they had choices of books and choices of activities. However, I liked that your board was focused on a specific author, so that all students had a common thread throughout their work. I teach fourth grade and have been looking for some higher level picture books to use for an author study and an online discussion forum. I've considered work by Patricia Polacco or Chris Van Allsburg, and I can see now how a choice board could be beneficial. I like that it can be made flexible enough that the same choice board can be used for multiple books.

—Laura (Colleague)

CHAPTER 4

CUBING

Overview

Cubing is an instructional strategy that has its roots in writing. The strategy uses a cube; on each face of the cube are directions using an action verb (such as create, compare, or analyze), and under each verb is a prompt providing a description of the task. Students roll the cube and complete the activity from the face of the cube that is turned up. They repeat this procedure until they have completed a total of six different tasks. Cubing can be used at any point in a lesson or unit. Like choice boards, cubing provides another way to differentiate instruction. Cubing is a novel way to structure a set of activities and to view a topic from multiple angles.

How and When to Use Cubing

Cubing is a versatile strategy that can easily fit into instructional plans at various points—beginning, middle, or end. A cube may be used to introduce a topic and find out what students already know. It may be used in sense-making activities or as a means of determining what students learned from a particular lesson or unit. Students may have their own individual cubes, or each group may be given a single cube. Cubes can be tiered to accommodate a variety of student cognitive abilities, skill levels, and knowledge of the topic. We have heard questions such as, "Couldn't you just list the activities on a sheet of paper and allow students to do the activities in any order?" Although you could certainly do that, we have found that students respond positively when we use strategies that are "fun." As you will see below, in the teacher comments, students who experienced cubing certainly thought it was a fun and exciting way to learn.

Directions for Making Cubes

Cubes are simple to design using the template provided here. Another alternative and a convenient way to acquire sturdy cubes is to purchase small (3 × 3 × 3) boxes from a packaging company. Printing the activities on mailing labels and affixing them to the box or template is easier than writing directly on either the box or the labels. If you choose to write directly on the cube, do so while the cube is unfolded, using a fine point, felt tip marker. The table function in a word processing program can also be used to create a cube. Form a 3 × 4 array, keep the first column and the middle row intact, and then delete the extraneous six cells. As another option, you may find it convenient to use The Dice Maker at http://www.toolsforeducators.com. No matter how you form the cube, the format for creating the activity on each face is the same: action verb + prompt.

How This Strategy Fits in the CIRCLE MAP

Cubes fit in the "differentiated instructional strategies" component of the CIRCLE MAP. They provide a simple yet lively means of varying the content, process, or product in a differentiated classroom.

Examples

The examples we have chosen address specific topics. These cubes were created by real teachers who have used them in their own classrooms. When possible, we have included comments from these teachers and their colleagues with the intention that their comments may provide additional insight into using the cubes. We have tried to include a wide variety of topics to give you a number of ideas for making your own cubes.

For example, Ashley Thompson attended a professional development workshop focusing on a variety of strategies that could be used to differentiate instruction. She particularly liked a strategy called cubing, but for her first attempt with her kindergartners, she decides to use one large cube, rather than giving a cube to each child. On a large, sturdy, 12 x 12 cube that she purchased from a mailing store, she pastes simple pictures of items such as a ball, a cat, a tree, and so forth until each face of the cube is covered. She then has the students stand in a circle. She places the cube in one student's hand and directs that student to say the name of the picture and its beginning letter sound. Once the student has completed the task, the student passes the cube to another student, turning it so that a different picture appears on top. The activity continues until all the faces have been used. Mrs. Thompson continues with the cube until each child has had a chance to participate, but she asks for new information each time a picture is reused. For example, she asks several students for the ending letter sounds featured on the box; other students she asks for rhyming words.

Template

Differentiation That Really Works (Grades K–2) © Prufrock Press Inc. • Permission is granted to photocopy or reproduce this page for classroom use only.

Cubing Activity for Similes

Argue for and against the use of similes.

Research and record the definition of the word *simile*.

Write a sentence or two using at least one simile.

Find an example of a simile in a story from one of the books in your book basket.

List as many similes as you can in 5 minutes.

Explain what it means if someone says, "You are as sharp as a tack."

Real Teacher Comments

The assignment we had with similes inspired this simile lesson for first grade. I am always trying to encourage the kids to throw a simile into their writing pieces. It is also important that they know what a simile is and notice that authors use them all the time. This activity took place with partners or small groups during writing time.

—Shannon Anderson (Teacher)

This activity would be effective at upper grade levels, too. May I "steal" it for my class?

—Sharon (Colleague)

I agree. This would be effective with my third/fourth graders as well.

—Megan (Colleague)

The idea of creating your cube based on similes was a great idea. You've included a lot of activities that are both thought provoking and creative. I would enjoy doing these activities if I were a student of yours. I especially like how you have students search for examples of similes (a great way for them to demonstrate their understanding and recognition of a simile) and have them "analyze" the meaning of a provided simile. Your activities provide students the opportunity to think and to really demonstrate their understanding of similes. Nice job!

—Rachel (Colleague)

I'd like to steal it, too. I didn't realize that first graders did similes, but they love the *Amelia Bedelia* books, so I'll bet they can do well with this.

—Diane (Colleague)

I think this activity would be really fun for the students in your class. It seems like a positive way to get them to take another look at similes.

—Heather (Colleague)

Topic: Civics and Government

Knowledge:
Visual
Draw and label three important members of your community.

Comprehension:
Visual
Make a Venn diagram showing the relationship between the rights and responsibilities of citizens of a community.

Application:
Written
Write a friendly letter to a parent summarizing the information you learned from the guest speaker from our county government.

Analysis:
Oral
Pretend you are running for office in our county government. Deliver a campaign speech that highlights the qualities you think a community leader should have.

Creative Thinking:
Kinesthetic
Imagine you live in a community without a government. In a small group, dramatize what life may be like.

Creative Thinking:
Written/Oral
Decide what age you think people should be able to vote. Justify your opinions in a written newspaper article or oral newscast.

Created by Barbara Katenkamp

Real Teacher Comments

This is a cube using the second-grade social studies standards for a civics and government unit. Students love the novelty and the choice. They were required to complete all of the activities. I used the Bloom's revised taxonomy and different learning styles for product options. I'd be happy to hear suggestions for improvement!

—Barbara Katenkamp (Teacher)

I really like your cube. As another second-grade teacher, I may have to borrow your cube when we get to that in social studies. I really like how you included using a friendly letter.

—Emily (Colleague)

CUBING–MATH
LEVEL i: Number Sense/Place Value

1. Count from 7 to 17.

2. Count from 4 to 25.

Read these number words to your partner:

two, six, ten, eight, nine, eleven, nineteen, fifteen

All of the numbers below are alike except for one. Which one is different? How is it different?

20 80 10 100

20 25 50 90

In your math notebook, write all of the ways to make 5. Use tallies, pictures, number sentences, and drawings.

Tom had 8 pennies. He gave some pennies away. He had 3 left. How many pennies did he give away? How did you figure it out?

In your math notebook, draw pictures to show these numbers:

25, 64, 19, 44

Tell the number of tens and ones for each number.

Created by Rhonda Brandt

CUBING—MATH
LEVEL 2: Number Sense/Place Value

Created by Rhonda Brandt

In your math notebook, write all of the ways to make 12. Use tallies, pictures, number sentences, and drawings.

Follow these steps to get to a number:

- Start with 2.
- Add 5.
- Add 20.
- Subtract 6.

Check with your partner. Did you get the same number?

Which number is different from the others? How is it different?

331   336   303

332   339   337

Count backward by 2's starting at 29. Have your partner check you. Write the numbers you say in your math notebook.

1. What number is 10 more than 59?

2. What number is 10 less than 75?

In your math notebook, draw pictures to show these numbers:

57   125   449

Tell the number of hundreds, tens, and ones for each number.

Real Teacher Comments

This is the first time I've used cubing in the classroom. I first met with small groups of students to introduce the activity and to make sure they understood how to do it. I then sent them off in pairs to work on the cubing activity. They really liked doing math in this way. I created two cubes based on readiness. I think a third may have been helpful. I tried to include multiple kinds of activities to peak interest.

—Rhonda Brandt (Teacher)

CUBE IT!

Created by Melinda Millholland

Knowledge

Using an organized list, list the main character and two other characters who are important to the plot development of *Frindle*.

Comprehension

Using an illustration, explain the problem in the book *Frindle*.

Application

Using a descriptive paragraph, summarize the plot.

Analysis

Using a Venn diagram, compare and contrast the main character in the book *Frindle* with the main character in the book *The Chocolate Touch*.

Creative Thinking

Using a storyboard, adapt the ending of *Frindle* to change the outcome. Write how it really ends on the back of the paper.

Critical Thinking

Write a friendly letter to me. In it, decide who should get credit for the creation of the word "frindle."

Real Teacher Comments

I used this assignment with my second graders as a comprehension test over the book *Frindle*. I told them they had to roll the die four times and respond to four of the activities. They really liked rolling the die, and they did fine with the questions.

—Melinda Millholland (Teacher)

I really liked the way you designed this activity with questions that model Bloom's taxonomy. You offer a nice variety of choices for them, too. I will add this activity to my file!

—Christine (Colleague)

I liked how you asked them to respond to four of the six sides of the cube. I bet your second graders liked the "chance" aspect of this activity.

—Sharon (Colleague)

This seems like a very engaging and provoking task for students. Your usage of Bloom's was great!

—Marlon (Colleague)

Wow! I sure am glad I chose to take a peek at your cubing activity, especially because I currently have a literature circle of third graders reading *Frindle*. As soon as they complete the book, I plan to borrow your creation as a means for extending their learning. Thanks!

—Gail (Colleague)

Activity Cube

Created by Jaci Greig

Remembering

Who were the three main characters in *The Case of the Back to School Burglar*? Who were some of the secondary characters?

Understanding

Choose two of the main characters. Using a Venn diagram, tell how they are alike and different.

Applying

The next story you will read is *The Case of the Missing Pumpkins*. How do you think it will be similar to *The Case of the Back to School Burglar*?

Analyzing

Look at the Calendar Club's newsletter at the end of the story. Read what each member of the club wrote, and tell why each person wrote what he or she did.

Evaluating

Explain what a red herring is and how some of the red herrings in this story made you think the burglar was someone other than Victoria.

Creating

Write an oath (promise) that members of Victoria's new club could take when they join her detective's club.

Real Teacher Comments

My first-grade groups enjoyed this activity more than the story map we started. Two of the groups were able to handle it just fine, as they are more mature and a little more settled. For the other two groups, the novelty revved them up a bit.

—Jaci Greig (Teacher)

Activity Cube

Created by Mandy Keele

Describe what type of genre this is, and explain how you know.

Summarize the responsibilities of one of the jobs listed in the story.

Discuss what kind of equipment you need to be a good student.

Write down two jobs where people make things (think of ones not in the story).

Act out what job you want to have when you grow up.

Write down two jobs that help people (think of ones not in the story).

Differentiation That Really Works (Grades K–2) © Prufrock Press Inc. • Permission is granted to photocopy or reproduce this page for classroom use only.

Real Teacher Comments

I used this cube for my first graders after we had read several stories about different jobs. The kids were very excited about them. They were in groups of four, so everyone had at least a couple of turns to roll. If they rolled something that they had already done, they just rolled again. While they were rolling, I was able to walk around and observe each group in action, because the activities on the cube didn't need much in the way of teacher guidance.

They particularly liked the one where they were able to act out what type of job they wanted to have when they were older. Before we ended the activity, if anyone hadn't gotten a chance to do that activity, he or she was given time to show his or her dramatic side.

I just used card stock to make the cubes this time, and after a round with first graders, they aren't in the best of shape. However, because this cube is pretty limited to these stories, longevity of the cubes was not as much of a concern. They are already asking me when we can do it again.

—Mandy Keele (Teacher)

I love when kids ask to do these kinds of activities again. Obviously, they enjoyed the experience. From now on, it is more like a game! I use my students' favorite learning activities as rewards for completion of tougher activities.

Because your class is into acting, maybe your next cube can have all different dramatic opportunities.

—Jason (Colleague)

"Rats on the Roof"

Created by Emily Kubek

Knowledge

What is an ad?

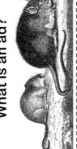

Application

What is the difference between on-the-surface questions and below-the-surface questions?

Analysis

Create a below-the-surface question for "Rats on the Roof."

Synthesis

Defend the rights of the rats.

Comprehension

Explain why the dogs place an ad for the cat.

Evaluation

Summarize what happens after the Tomcat runs out of the house screaming.

Real Teacher Comments

This story is from the advanced level reader book for Theme 1 in the Houghton Mifflin Language Arts book for second graders. The book is actually a collection of stories, but the first one is called "Rats on the Roof." I talked about Bloom's verbs as I introduced the cube.

The students enjoyed doing the cube activity. I told them that they would be doing the activity after they read the story. It seemed to make them more engaged in what they were reading, because they knew that they were going to have to answer questions when they were finished. The questions really made some of them think about what had happened in the story, as well as what could have happened if the situation had been different.

—Emily Kubek (Teacher)

I like how you used Bloom's!

—Alicia (Colleague)

I have never heard of it. We sometimes get into philosophical questions, and it sounds like there are at least two perspectives with this book.

—Roberta (Colleague)

This would help them be more engaged in their reading. Did they see the questions before they read the story?

—Loretta (Colleague)

I'm also wondering if you showed the students the cube before they read the book. I wonder if you would get different results if you showed them, as opposed to not. Do you think they'd think differently?

—Kristen (Colleague)

They did not see the questions before they read the story; however, we talked about some things as the story was being read. They did know that there was the cube with questions; they just did not know what they were going to be!

—Emily (Teacher)

Science—What Is Matter?

Give an example of a **gas.**

Give an example of a **solid.**

Locate an object in the room. Describe two of its **properties.**

What is **matter?**

Name the three states of **matter.**

Give an example of a **liquid.**

Real Teacher Comments

I have done cubes with other groups in the past. Those cubes have been language based—who, what, when type questions; vocabulary words; and story starters. This time I designed a cube to go with our science lesson. The second graders have been learning about states of matter and describing properties of matter. As a review, instead of having them complete the worksheet that accompanied the lesson, I made a cube asking the same types of questions found on the worksheet. I placed the students in groups of three, and they took turns rolling the cube and answering the questions. I circulated around the room taking a formative assessment to check for student understanding. The students enjoyed doing the activity, and I liked being able to listen to their responses.

—Julia Lester (Teacher)

I like this cube. I think the best part about it is that no matter how many times a side comes up, it allows for students to create a unique response, especially if you made it a rule that you can't use an answer more than once. Then they would really have to pay close attention.

—Daniel (Colleague)

I agree—the idea of not being able to use an answer more than once makes kids think, and you get into some creative thinking, rather than the obvious. Great idea, and I bet the students enjoyed the activity more than writing down answers to the questions. The cube tends to turn work into a game, and what kid doesn't enjoy that?

—Kimberly (Colleague)

Cube for High-Ability Learners

List places where you might find a pattern.

Use what you know about an AB pattern to create an ABB and ABC pattern.

Describe what a pattern is and give an example.

Use the enclosed pieces to complete the patterns.

Why are patterns so important?

Decide which pattern you could complete. What is wrong with the other one?

Cube for Grade-Level Learners

Use the enclosed pieces to complete the patterns.

How do you know what comes next in a pattern?

Decide which pattern you could complete.

What is a pattern?

Use what you know about an AB pattern to create an AB pattern for the class.

Find an AB pattern in or around our classroom.

Created by Alicia Mathis

Real Teacher Comments

I worked really hard to create leveled cubes for patterning in kindergarten. I really liked the idea of enclosing items inside the cube. I have small pattern puzzles of varying ability levels, which would be perfect to place in each one. This took a little more work than I thought it was going to, but it is a wonderful tool to have now!

—Alicia Mathis (Teacher)

I really liked your cubes on patterning. This is a great opportunity for you to put materials inside the cube.

—Emily (Colleague)

I loved your cube for kindergarten. I was amazed at the level of questions they could answer. The fact that items are inside the cube just makes this activity more exciting. I think I'll try putting something inside the cube for my students next time.

—Suzanne (Colleague)

Putting pattern puzzles in each cube is a great idea!

—Loretta (Colleague)

This is really interesting, and it looks really high level for kindergarten students.

—Billie (Colleague)

I'm sure it was hard for you to create activities for your little ones. Even though the activities are appropriate for this age, I'm sure you have to help them read the cube, explain the activity, help with taking turns, help them stay on task, and so on! That makes this activity a bit more challenging, I'm sure.

—Christina (Colleague)

You always have such cute kindergarten ideas. I like your idea of placing the items inside. That definitely adds some interest. I may have to try this when we get to shapes. Nice job!

—Sandra (Colleague)

I agree. I love your kindergarten things. I have borrowed a few of them and adapted them to fit my first graders!

—Debra (Colleague)

I used the cubes with three of my center groups today. Things went pretty well! I probably could have used a third one for my lowest kids. I will work on that for the next time I use it. My high kids did very well with all of the activities, especially the one that has them apply AB to ABB and ABC. They loved the choices and the fact that it was a cube.

—Alicia (Teacher)

Activity Cube

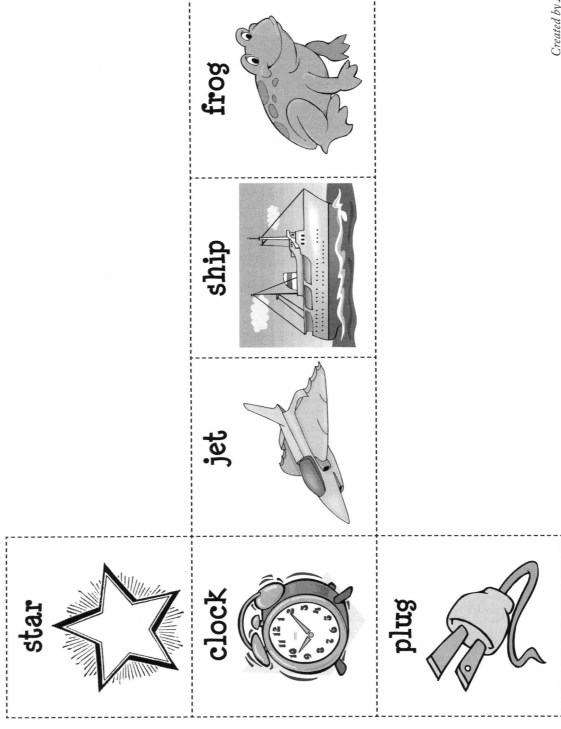

star

clock

plug

jet

ship

frog

Differentiation That Really Works (Grades K–2) © Prufrock Press Inc. • Permission is granted to photocopy or reproduce this page for classroom use only.

Real Teacher Comments

This cube is for my kindergarten classroom and is on rhyming words. Students rolled the cube, said the word, and then had to produce a rhyming word. Students were not allowed to duplicate answers. As a student said the word, we added that word to a list on the board, so that in the end we had a list of six word families. It was neat to see how students began to pick up on the spelling patterns as they added words to the lists.

The kids LOVED this activity. Anything that seems like a game is always a hit with kindergarten kids. We have been working on rhyming words all year, but there are still a few who struggle with this. It was nice to have a different approach to practice this skill. It gave me an additional opportunity to do a quick assessment.

—Ashley Peters (Teacher)

I like that you wrote the words down on the board for the students to see. I do have a couple of questions about your experience:

Did you write all of the words from the cube on the board first, or did you add them to the board as the students rolled the word initially?

What was your board set-up for displaying the rhyming words? Did you make columns on the board for each of the cube words?

—Erin (Colleague)

I did write all of the words from the cube across the board before we started, and then we created a list under each word. I purposely had the kids who I knew would struggle go first, so this took out some of the frustration of having to think of a word that no one had said. It was definitely more difficult for the kids who went last, but they were the kids who were up for the challenge.

—Ashley (Teacher)

This was a great piece for an assessment, and I really like the idea of making it a rhyming game for the students and listing the words on the board. I'm sure it's easier for those visual learners to grasp the concept when they start seeing the spelling patterns line up. I may have to borrow this idea!

—Kimberly (Colleague)

Activity Cube

Enhancement Expert

What is one thing you could change on this item to make it better?

Application Analyzer

What is this item used for?

Radical Relater

How does this relate to or remind you of something else? What else is like this item?

Exploration Station

Create a list of 10 sentences that describe what you are looking at.

Mechanics Master

How is this put together?

Creation Captain

How could this item be used for something other than its intended use?

Real Teacher Comments

I used this cube as part of my center time to promote critical thinking. My students explored a Matchbox car. Other fun items I would use for this activity would be a telephone or a flashlight.

—Tamara Weller (Teacher)

CHAPTER 5

GRAPHIC ORGANIZERS

Overview

Graphic organizers are visual tools used by teachers to assist students in analyzing, interpreting, and making sense of the content. Graphic organizers come in many forms, depending on their use. Examples include Venn diagrams, compare/contrast charts, double bubble diagrams, and flow charts. Graphic organizers can be used as advanced organizers, as sense-making activities, or as formative or summative assessments.

How and When to Use Graphic Organizers

Graphic organizers are often used as advanced organizers at the beginning of a lesson or activity to assist students in understanding the content. They also may be used for practice with activities that require students to make sense of the content. The teacher might choose to use graphic organizers to gather formative or summative data. To accommodate the needs of all learners, some organizers may be blank, while others may be partially completed, depending on the readiness level of the students.

Directions for Making Graphic Organizers

Graphic organizers are simple to design. However, there is no set template. The form and function of the graphic organizer will depend on the topic being taught, as well as the thinking skills students will be using. Inspiration®

is one type of software that can be used to create graphic organizers (http://www.inspiration.com).

How This Strategy Fits in the CIRCLE MAP

When used for assessment purposes, graphic organizers fit into the "differentiated assessment" component of the CIRCLE MAP. However, when used as advanced organizers or sense-making activities, they fit into the "differentiated instructional strategies" component.

Examples

The examples we have chosen include specific graphic organizers, as well as those that can be readily adapted to many topics. These organizers were created by real teachers who have used them in their own classrooms. When possible, we have included comments from these teachers and their colleagues with the intention that their comments may provide additional insight into using the organizers.

For example, in Mr. O'Rourke's first-grade language arts class, the students are reviewing "beginning, middle, and end" in the stories they have recently read. He has designed a graphic organizer to assist the students in identifying these elements. The graphic organizer has three big boxes, each about 3 x 6. The left side of the box is flush with the left side of the paper, and the longer portion extends toward the other side of the paper. The first box has the word "First" written in it with space left for writing a response. The box below has "Next" written in it, and the last box contains the word "Finally." Mr. O'Rourke provides the names of several stories from which students may choose for the activity. Students complete the graphic organizer while Mr. O'Rourke walks around the room to get a good idea of which students seem to have mastered the concept and who might still need some reteaching. Once the students have completed the graphic organizers, he has them move into groups based on the stories they used to complete the activity, and then they share their results.

Template

Due to the nature of graphic organizers, there is no universal template.

Power Writing Umbrella

Power 1: Main Idea

Power 2: Major supporting ideas that talk about the Power 1

Power 1: School Supplies

Power 2:   Pencils

Power 2:   Scissors

Power 2:   _____

Power 2:   _____

Created by Mandy Keele

Real Teacher Comments

With my first graders, I usually wait until the second semester to introduce them to power writing. During the first semester, we tend to focus more on word choice, sentence variety, voice, and conventions. Anyway, now that we're getting into the organizational piece, I introduced them to the power writing umbrella this week. We've talked about the main idea and the supporting details/ideas in reading, so they're familiar with those terms. The first umbrella that they viewed had the Power I (PI) and Power 2 (P2) provided for them as an example. Subsequent examples were missing either some P2's, PI's, or both. Once we had finished the examples, we brainstormed a list of possible PI's.

As they were working independently to create their own umbrellas, I was quickly able to pinpoint those children who still needed help and pull them into a smaller group. As the other children finished, they worked with a partner stating one of their Power 2's, and the partner had to try and guess the Power I. (Can you guess it with one P2? Can you guess it with two? Did you need three? Did you need all four?) Needless to say, they loved this! The PI's ranged from Pokemon, to favorite books, to best light saber duels (from a total *Star Wars* fanatic). Next they'll choose one of their umbrellas for a writing activity. I really like having this electronically now, and the children loved the interactive component using the SmartBoard.

—Mandy Keele (Teacher)

Wow! Power writing! The one thing I did like about that program was the organizer, specifically for informative writing. It really helped some of my students who could not organize their thoughts on paper. I remember personally feeling like the program was heavily involved in a "process" with all of the PI's and P2's. However, in terms of a graphic organizer, this is a great example of showing students ways to organize their thoughts!

—Jennifer (Colleague)

Mandy, I think any time you can make an activity revolve more around the kids' interests, it goes so much better! This looks like a cool activity, even though I'm not familiar with power writing. And to double it with using the SmartBoard—I bet those kids were just eating it up! Nice job motivating them.

—Adrienne (Colleague)

This is a great graphic organizer! I'm sure the kids loved it, especially when they had the opportunity to share their Power 2's with a partner. Any time you can turn learning into a game for kids, they will be more engaged. I also love how you incorporated technology by using the Smartboard.

—Ashley (Colleague)

Go to Writing View to add details.

Use pictures and words to show how life today is different from the way it was long ago.

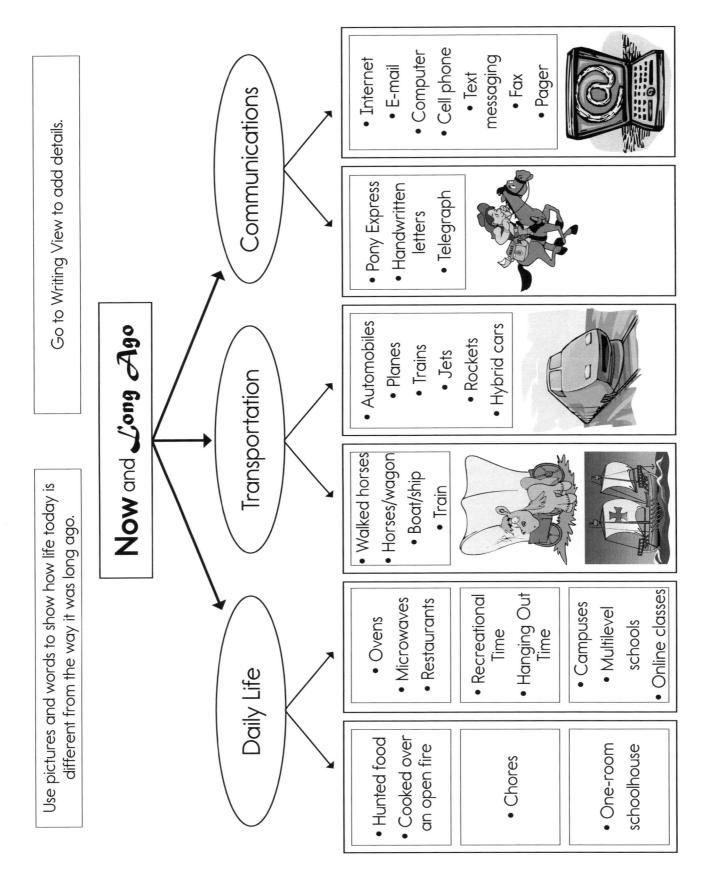

Now and *Long Ago*

Communications

- Internet
- E-mail
- Computer
- Cell phone
- Text messaging
- Fax
- Pager

- Pony Express
- Handwritten letters
- Telegraph

Transportation

- Automobiles
- Planes
- Trains
- Jets
- Rockets
- Hybrid cars

- Walked horses
- Horses/wagon
- Boat/ship
- Train

Daily Life

- Ovens
- Microwaves
- Restaurants

- Recreational Time
- Hanging Out Time

- Campuses
- Multilevel schools
- Online classes

- Hunted food
- Cooked over an open fire

- Chores

- One-room schoolhouse

Created by Vicki Heil

Real Teacher Comments

Graphic organizers are fantastic! I have found that second graders have an extremely hard time focusing, and when asked to write about a particular topic, they kind of ricochet all over the place. I have 21 second graders, and my room is considered a gifted cluster classroom. Graphic organizers really help. The unit we are working on now is called "Now and Long Ago." We have Kidspiration 2 in our computer lab. After reading the small amount of material in our book, we studied other material in more depth, such as the Pony Express, the Oregon Trail, and Paul Revere's ride. Then we went to the lab, and each student got to use the template attached to fill in some ideas. It held each child responsible for pulling together what had been learned. It was also a small step toward the larger one of writing a nice paper about "Now and Long Ago."

We are in the process of writing now, but we are not finished. Already, I have seen better and lengthier work than I feel I would have gotten had I not used the graphic organizer.

Some things I noticed: Some students were frustrated with the limited space to write in the boxes, and a few spent too much time looking for pictures. On a positive note, some got very creative. Also, kids love to look over and check out their neighbors' screens, and when they saw someone with a long list, it inspired them to try to think of more. That's a good thing!

—Vicki Heil (Teacher)

I really liked your graphic organizer. I agree that second graders have trouble staying focused. I teach a literacy group and have a pull-out group of second graders once a week. I am going to be focusing on states of matter with my pull-out group. I plan this time to use some type of graphic organizer. The graphic organizer will be a great way for the students to see the differences in gases, liquids, and solids.

—Julia (Colleague)

I also teach second grade, so I always enjoy looking at what you have done with your class. This is a great graphic organizer. The organizer kept them focused while doing their research. I'm sure the finished products will reflect time well spent using your chart. I have noticed that when I use some type of organizer before writing, my students do a much better job getting their information across in their papers.

—Maura (Colleague)

Created by Christine Gesse

Five Senses

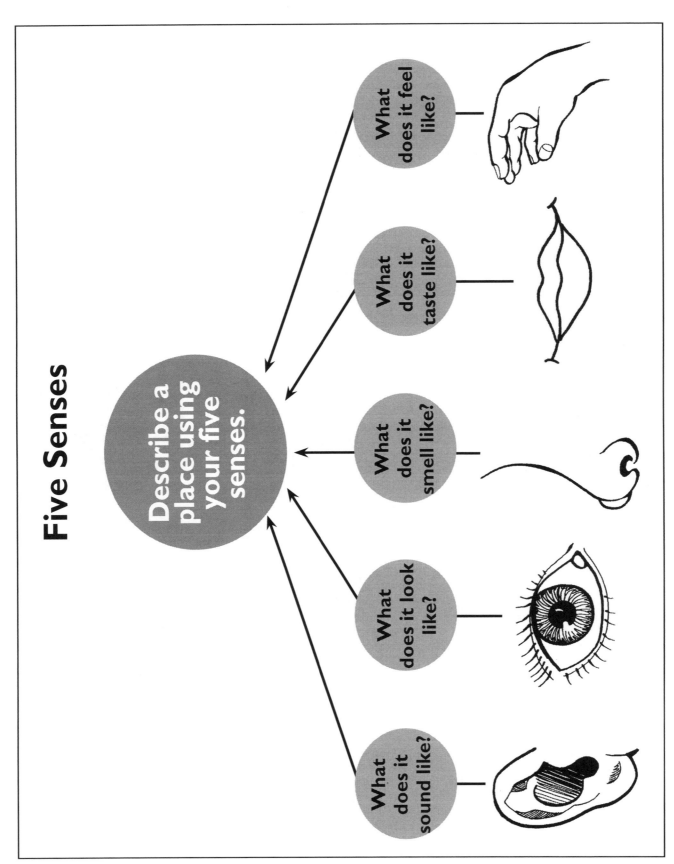

Real Teacher Comments

I asked my students to write a description of their favorite places. The results were dreadful! Many wrote about the place where they play video games and used the plain words: cool, fun, and nice. I then used an overhead of the graphic organizer, and as a class, we filled in the senses that described our tree house. Students got the idea quickly and all agreed that the reading became more interesting. Next, students were given their own organizers and the opportunity to either keep or change their topics in the rewrite. They were really excited to try this, and I could tell when they thought of something special.

—Christine Gesse (Teacher)

I like your senses organizer. It could be used for a variety of purposes (e.g., writing or science). Like you, I have writing projects turn out poorly when we don't do some sort of organizational prewriting. It is a good lesson learned.

—Sharon (Colleague)

What a great idea! I can see where that concept could be adapted for math to help with solving word problems, steps for solving equations, and what I call "reading the problem" (not a word problem—just a regular math problem). So many new ideas to try!

—Julie (Colleague)

Your graphic organizer would certainly appeal to the second graders, especially the color and the graphics. I am sure some of the students were able to add some quality details to their narratives as a result of your prewriting activity. Having the children think about the information drawn in by their senses was a good way to connect their emotions to their writing.

—Gail (Colleague)

I've found that graphic organizers really help my first graders with prewriting for writing projects. I like how your graphics really jump out at you as a reminder to include all of the senses.

—Kristen (Colleague)

Created by Jaci Greig

Vocabulary Graphic Organizer

Draw a picture of your word or a symbol that represents your word.

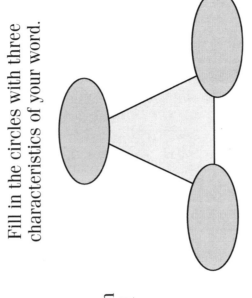

Fill in the circles with three characteristics of your word.

If the vocabulary word were part of an answer, what would the question be?

Write your word here

_____

List three nonexamples of your word.

1. _____

2. _____

3. _____

Complete an analogy using your word. Be sure to explain how the items in each set are related.

_____ as _____

Explain the relationship: _____

Real Teacher Comments

We have several teachers who are new to our cluster program this year, and I am mentoring two new teachers. A recurring theme in our professional discussions is that students are having difficulty with content vocabulary, specifically math. I plan to give the organizer to these teachers. There will need to be some preteaching before the students will be able to independently complete these. They will need to be familiar with analogies and the particular format of writing them that is on the organizer. There will also need to be some modeling and practicing of the "nonexample" concept. Once those items are addressed, I hope this organizer is generic enough that it will be able to be used with any subject. To compose this, I took items from Marzano's vocabulary work and the Frayer model.

—Jaci Greig (Teacher)

TOMORROW'S ALPHABET

Brainstorm words that start with your letter:

fog	flag	forever	freedom
fire	forest	farm	feature
fat	fawn	frown	fever
fear	figure	friend	feet
future	feast	flea	fly
flock	fort	flute	Frankenstein

Today's _____ is	tomorrow's _____.
tadpole	frog
war	freedom
ingredients, harvest, groceries	feast
minnow	fish
snowball fight	fever
enemy	friend
wood	fire
calories, desserts	fat
distraction	failure
blankets, snow	fort
misunderstanding	fight

Final Decision:
Today's snowball fight is tomorrow's fever.

TOMORROW'S ALPHABET

Brainstorm words that start with your letter:

[blank box]

Today's _____ is   tomorrow's _____.

[lined writing area]

Final Decision:

Created by Erin Mohr

Real Teacher Comments

If you're not familiar with *Tomorrow's Alphabet,* it's a great book in which the author really makes the reader think about what's to come and make predictions. It's such a good addition to a unit on change, because each letter stands for what something will become in the future. There are simple ones in the book (D is for puppy—tomorrow's dog) and more complex ones (E is for campfire—tomorrow's embers). I designed a graphic organizer that we could use to make a class book. We did the graphic organizer together on the projector first so they would understand it. Then each child did his or her own for a particular letter. I think the graphic organizer helped them use higher level thinking to create better connections than they would have if they'd just had to make one pop out of their heads. (I would probably have received a lot more D is for puppies!) I included the one we did as a class and the blank one as well.

—Erin Mohr (Teacher)

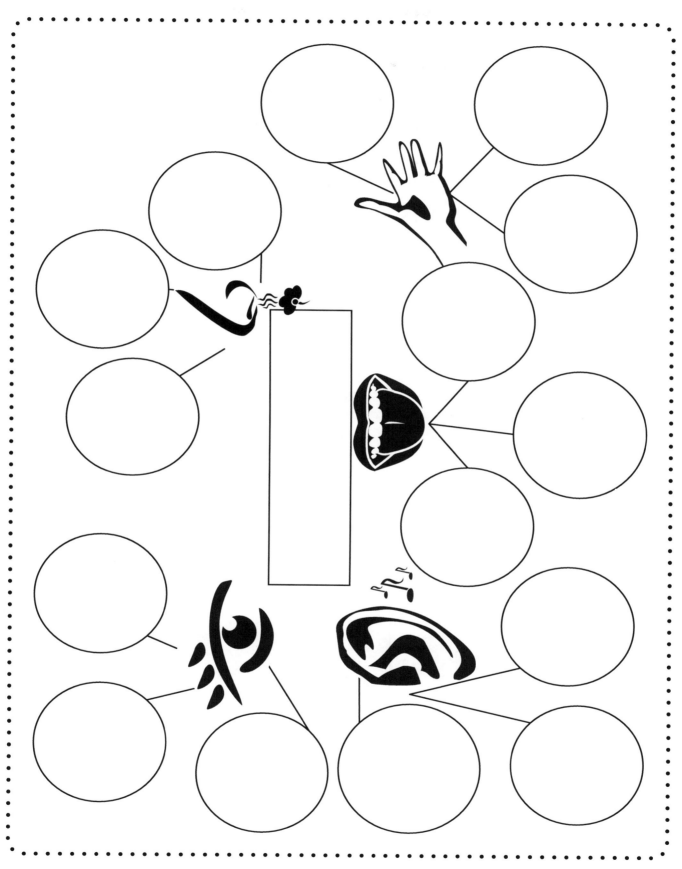

Real Teacher Comments

I taught an art lesson using Paul Cezanne's "Still Life of Cherries and Peaches." The students did a 30-second look, and then we talked about it. They pretended they were inside the painting. We talked about what room they could be in and what they could be hearing, smelling, feeling, tasting, and seeing. After we shared these things for a few minutes, I had the students go back to their seats to complete this graphic organizer on the five senses. They were able to look back at the painting if they needed to. I wanted them to fit short phrases or words into each bubble. One student drew pictures in his as well. The students really seemed to like this activity. They enjoyed being able to pretend they were there in the room of the painting. They were able to share a lot of their answers with me, and the discussion could have lasted a lot longer than the time we had for it!

—Emily Kubek (Teacher)

I have used a table chart similar to this, but I like this better. The visuals will help younger children remember what sense they are working on. The graphic organizer is flexible enough to use with many subjects.

—Alicia (Colleague)

I can see how the kids would associate the ideas better with the graphics!

—Debra (Colleague)

This graphic organizer is very versatile. It could be used in language arts to help kids describe something using more details before writing a story. It could be used in science when doing lab work or when observing new things. I really like how it could go many different ways.

—Nichole (Colleague)

Story Event Organizer

Today you read a story about a letter person. In the three boxes below, please record the first event that happened in the story, the middle event that happened in the story, and the last event that happened in the story. Please draw a picture of each event. There are also lines for writing words to describe each event. Use your sounds!

1 **2** **3**

Created by Melissa Yekulis

Real Teacher Comments

This graphic organizer is one I use with my kindergarten students. After reading the story of the week to the class, I invited them to draw (and write if they were able) the three main events of the story, in order. This way, I could check for comprehension, as well as for their understanding of sequence of events.
—Melissa Yekulis (Teacher)

You could use one or two as a center activity. Laminate them and then cut them apart and let students put them in the correct order. You could photocopy the original as an answer key for self-checking. I would probably code them somehow, because you know they would get mixed in together.
—Sharon (Colleague)

I really like this idea for a concept map. This is something that I could use in my Spanish classes. We are always reading (usually short dialogues or really short stories). This would be a great way for my students to demonstrate their reading comprehension abilities and summarization skills using Spanish that they know!
—Rachel (Colleague)

Name:_____ Date:_____

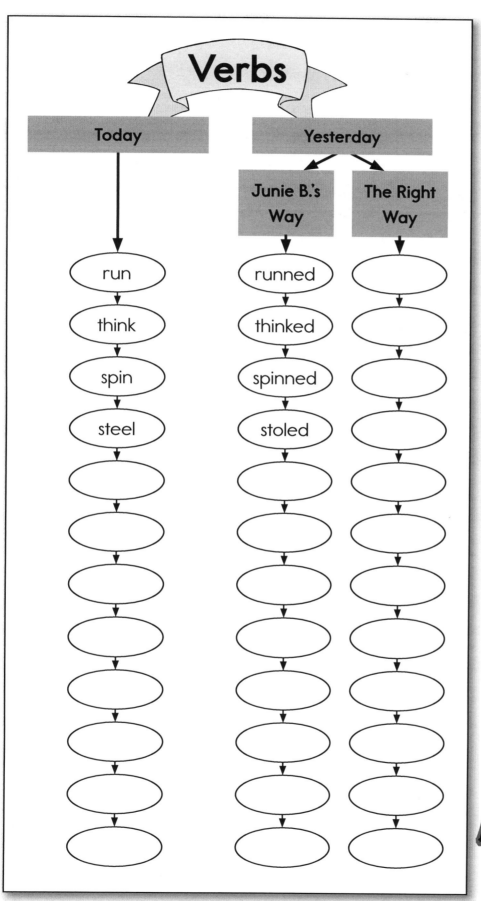

Verbs

Today	Yesterday	
	Junie B.'s Way	The Right Way
run	runned	
think	thinked	
spin	spinned	
steel	stoled	

Junie B. doesn't always use verbs the correct way when she tells a story. Write the correct forms of the verb in the bubbles on the right. As you read, look for more of Junie B.'s verbs and add them to your list.

Created by Allison Gill

Real Teacher Comments

My first-grade reading group is reading *Junie B. Jones Is Not a Crook*. On Wednesday, I introduced the word "verb" in place of "action word." We also talked about how Junie B. doesn't always use verbs the right way. She likes to just put "ed" on the ends of many irregular verbs. I thought the graphic organizer would be a good way to help students hunt for the incorrect verbs in the story.

—Allison Gill (Teacher)

I have always liked Junie B., but I was always worried about the verbs being used incorrectly. It is important to point out to students that she doesn't always talk correctly so they don't start to mimic her (they will do that in first grade).

—Lindy (Colleague)

There are so many lessons to be learned from Junie B. I'm also thinking that it might be a good activity to use with some of our older special needs students. Because some of them read at this level, it would be a nice excuse to be using these books. As a matter of fact, we do a picture book activity in sixth grade and could use this idea in conjunction with that as well.

—Quella (Colleague)

How-To Organizer

How to: TASk	Step 1:
	Step 2:
	Step 3:
	Step 4:
	Step 5:
	Step 6:

Created by Sharon Boggs

Real Teacher Comments

I use this graphic organizer as a prewriting assignment to help my students think through a task, such as building a snowman. Using a word processor or KidSpiration, they can modify their work easily if they think of an additional step or get one out of order, such as writing "put the carrot on the top ball for the snowman's nose" before they have mentioned putting the top ball on the body.

—Sharon Boggs (Teacher)

I can see that it can be used for many topics and grade levels. I also like that you could put sequential words in the boxes for kids who have trouble organizing, such as first, next, then, after that, and finally. Thanks for sharing!

—Sam (Colleague)

I can see how this could be used for visualizing math rules such as how to solve equations and how to solve word problems. I can also see it being used in a slightly different format for older students to assist them with planning certain projects that we have during the semester.

—Julie (Colleague)

Character or Event Description Chart

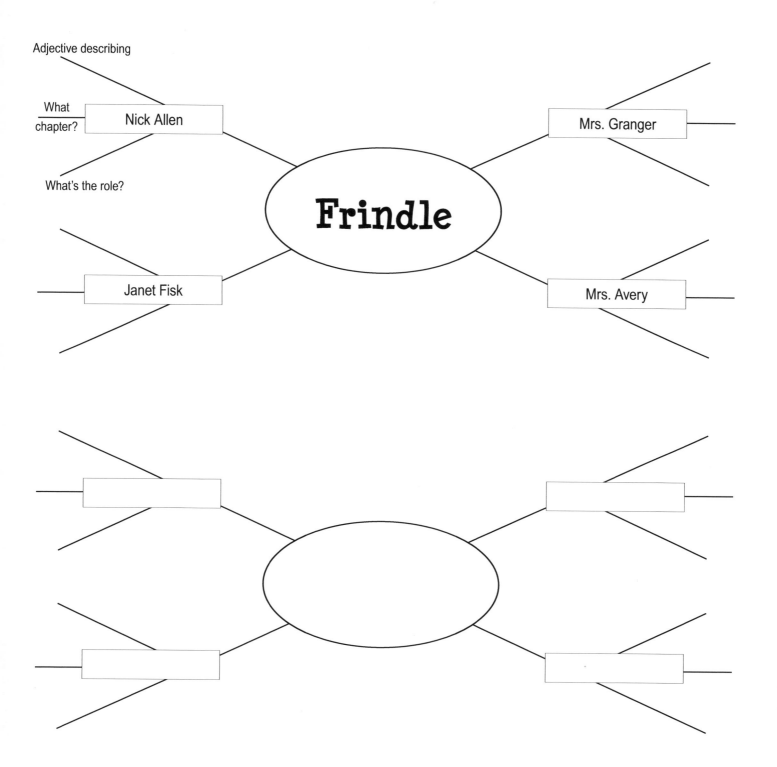

Adjective describing

What
chapter?

Nick Allen

What's the role?

Janet Fisk

Frindle

Mrs. Granger

Mrs. Avery

Created by Melinda Millholland

Real Teacher Comments

I used this graphic organizer with my students in my gifted second-grade class. It was a way for them to organize the characters in the book *Frindle*. I had them give the character's name, an adjective to describe the character, in what chapter they first appeared, and the character's role (e.g., teacher, student). We have been working a lot with character, plot, and setting, so this came in handy.

—Melinda Millholland (Teacher)

This organizer could be used with many different forms of literature. It is a good way for students to keep the characters organized so they don't get confused about roles or characteristics.

—Karen (Colleague)

all

Created by Debra Raines

Real Teacher Comments

I first modeled this organizer to the class with the "all" word family. Then, I gave students their own blank "et" word family graphic organizers to fill out. The kids really got it and knew just what to do. Then, to my surprise, later in the day, the kids were using what they had remembered and applying the words to different lessons.

—Debra Raines (Teacher)

Sometimes all it takes is one activity like this to make a connection with the children! I'm glad that it worked and that they applied what they learned to their work later in the day.

—Loretta (Colleague)

It is not always easy to think about how to use a graphic organizer with really young children. You must have done a great job modeling for them.

—Roberta (Colleague)

What a great way to teach the concept of graphic organizers to young children!

—Kristin (Colleague)

Name:_____ Date:_____

| Use pictures and words |
| to tell about your animal. |

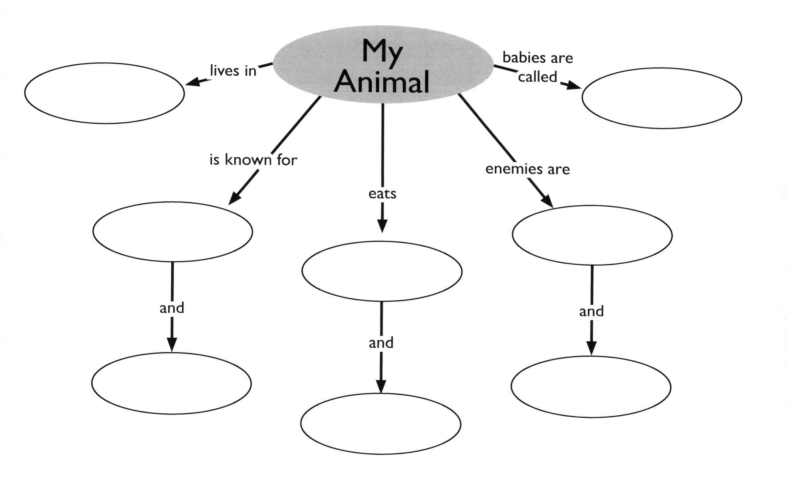

lives in

My Animal

babies are called

is known for

eats

enemies are

and

and

and

Created by Ali Wade

Real Teacher Comments

My students completed this and then had to present it in front of the class. I have a laptop hooked to my doc-cam, and they stood up by the screen and gave their presentations while showing models they made of their ocean creatures. They loved it!

—Ali Wade (Teacher)

What a great idea of using the organizer as a launch for an oral presentation! What a good way for kids to have notes for a "speech" without fumbling for note cards. It looks professional and is authentic—just like a CEO giving a PowerPoint presentation!

—Mona (Colleague)

CHAPTER 6

LEARNING CONTRACTS

Overview

Learning contracts are "bargains" between the teacher and a student or group of students. Learning contracts may be on any topic and may be considered abbreviated lesson plans or mini-units. That is, learning contracts list standards, concepts, goals, activities, resources, products, and assessments in a format that is student-friendly. They have a starting and an ending date and a place for the student, the teacher, and the student's parents to sign indicating that the contract is binding. Generally, learning contracts are used as an alternative to regular instruction, especially when students have been compacted out of a portion of the curriculum.

How and When to Use Learning Contracts

In a classroom, the learners are at various levels of readiness. To accommodate these differences, many teachers begin a unit of instruction by pre-testing the entire class on the planned content. Some students may already know significant portions of the content and need alternative activities while the rest of the class proceeds with learning the content that is new to them. To provide clearly articulated learning experiences for the students who have already mastered the planned content, a learning contract is often an appropriate choice. Generally, the student and teacher jointly plan the contract, agree to its terms, and sign it. In our experience, it is also vital that parents sign the contract to avoid unnecessary miscommunication.

Directions for Making Learning Contracts

Learning contracts are simple to create using the template provided below. However, it is also easy to design your own learning contract in order to customize it to a particular topic. Any learning contract should include all of the elements of the template.

How This Strategy Fits in the CIRCLE MAP

A learning contract fits in the "differentiated instructional strategies" component of the CIRCLE MAP. Learning contracts are generally alternative assignments used to accommodate individuals or small groups, rather than whole-class learning needs.

Examples

The examples we have chosen all use the template, but address different topics. These contracts were created by real teachers who have used them in their own classrooms. When possible, we have included comments from these teachers and their colleagues with the intention that their comments may provide additional insight into using the learning contract and creating your own or another topic.

For example, Mei-lee, Eric, and Jada are students in Ellen Caldwell's second-grade math class. The next topic in math focuses on geometry, specifically shapes. On a pretest over that topic, Mrs. Caldwell found that most of her class had only a rudimentary knowledge of the topic. The exceptions were Mei-lee, Eric, and Jada. All three scored 97% to 100% on the pretest. She meets with these three students to discuss possible options for a learning contract for their use during the time when other students will be learning about shapes. From a list of topics, all three students find tangrams to be an exciting topic. Together with the students, Mrs. Caldwell constructs a contract that focuses on the book *Grandfather Tang's Story*. She helps the students identify other books, videos, and websites that might be helpful. She ties the objectives to state standards and develops the contract, making sure to include check points to ensure the students are on target with their independent work. The students will learn about tangrams and their history, make their own tangram sets, and use them to solve various spatial problems. Once developed, each contract is signed by the student, his or her parents, and Mrs. Caldwell.

Template

Title of Learning Contract

Standards:

Goals/Objectives:

Topic:

Activities:

Resources:

Product/Outcome:

Evaluation Criteria:

Signatures:

Student: _____   Teacher: _____

Parent: _____   Date: _____

Learning Contract for Second Grade Math

Name: _____

Date Started: _____ Date Due: _____

Progress Check: _____

Progress Check: _____

This contract replaces all of the regular class work on the concept of time.

During math, I will complete the activities listed below. When I am done, I will participate in a discussion with my teacher and other contract participants about the activities I completed.

_____1. Create a poster that explains how to read both a digital and an analog clock.

_____2. There are several time zones throughout the U.S. Prepare a PowerPoint presentation that describes the reasons for time zones and the locations/borders of the time zones throughout the U.S. You may need to access the Internet or go to the library.

_____3. Our school day begins at 9 a.m. and ends at 3:30 p.m. Think about all of the components that go into creating a schedule. Complete your own weekly school schedule. You may use the attached chart to help you get started. (Be sure to schedule lunch, recess, special classes, and literature groups.)

_____4. Use the movie schedule from the newspaper (provided) to create a daylong movie marathon. Analyze the movie times from one theatre location and create a schedule that allows you to see the most movies in one day. (Rule: You may not leave one movie for another.)

_____5. People in Indiana feel very strongly about Daylight Saving Time (DST). Interview three adults to find out their opinions about DST. Write up a summary of each interview.

I realize that I must work independently during math and not interrupt others. I must use my time and resources wisely.

Student Signature: _____

Teacher Signature: _____

Parent Signature: _____

It's About Time

Standards:

- Tell time to the nearest half-hour and relate time to events (before/after, shorter/longer).

- Use tools such as objects or drawings to model problems.

- Make precise calculations and check the validity of the results in the context of the problem.

Resources needed: access to the library, access to the Internet, notebook paper, worksheet with grid, newspaper with movie times, poster board

Grid for Activity 3

Times	Monday	Tuesday	Wednesday	Thursday	Friday

Created by Sharon Boggs

Real Teacher Comments

I really like the idea of using a learning contract with my high-ability first graders. This strategy fosters independence, which is often difficult for my young students, and allows students to work deeper into the concept we are studying.

—Sharon Boggs (Teacher)

I particularly like the way you are allowing children who already know how to tell time to have the opportunity to USE time. Nice job!

—Dawn (Colleague)

Independent Learning Contract
First-Grade Enrichment Group Student

Name: _____

Subject: Reading

Date Started: _____ **Completion Due:** _____

Standards:

- Read aloud fluently and accurately with appropriate changes in voice and expression.
- Use titles, tables of contents, and chapter headings to locate information in a text.
- Compare plots, settings, or characters presented by different authors.
- Write a friendly letter complete with the date, salutation, body, closing, and signature.

Goals/Objectives:

- Students will be able to independently read above-grade-level fiction books in the mystery genre.
- Students will be able to recognize the relationship between chapter titles and information contained in the chapters.
- Students will be able to compare plots, settings, and/or characters in different stories.
- Students will be able to write a friendly letter to a character in one of the stories they have read.

Activities:

Due Dates for Activities	Activities for Students to Complete	Student Initials	Parent Initials	Teacher Initials
	Read *The Case of the Missing Pumpkins*. Practice reading some chapters in your head, and read some aloud with the Whisper-Ma-Phone.			
	Complete the worksheet about chapter titles and main events.			
	Complete a story map for *The Case of the Missing Pumpkins* like we did for *The Case of the Back-to-School Burglar*.			
	Use your story maps to compare and contrast the two stories using a Venn diagram. Write a letter to one of the main characters in the books (Casey, Leon, or Dottie). Tell him or her why you would like to be his or her friend or why you would like to be a member of the Calendar Club.			

Resources:
- Two books from the Calendar Club Mysteries series, *The Case of the Back-to-School Burglar* and *The Case of the Missing Pumpkin*
- Whisper-Ma-Phones for reading aloud to yourself quietly
- Worksheet on chapter titles and main events for *The Case of the Missing Pumpkins*
- Venn diagram template
- Friendly letter template and friendly letter example

Product/Outcome:
- Students will complete a story map after reading *The Case of the Missing Pumpkins*.
- Students will complete a Venn diagram to compare and contrast two stories from the same genre of fiction.
- Students will write a friendly letter to a story character.

Evaluation Criteria:
- Students will be able to compare and contrast the two mystery stories they have read.
- Given a chapter title, students will be able to predict what kind of event or information might be contained in that chapter.
- Students will be able to complete a story map after reading a short book.
- Students will exhibit improved fluency as demonstrated in a DIBELS check.
- Students will be able to write a friendly letter using the correct letter parts.

Common Understandings:
- I understand that the work described in the boxes will be completed independently.
- I understand that the work will act as a substitute for some learning stations in the classroom.
- I understand that the books used in this contract may be read during independent reading time.

Signatures:

Student: _____

Teacher: _____

Parent: _____

Created by Jaci Greig

Real Teacher Comments

The learning contract I have created was used with first graders who are reading well above grade level, so I targeted second-grade standards for them. I met once a week with these students. They completed the contract during independent reading time or station time when the stations were alphabetic principle, fluency, sight words, and so forth.

The activities I included required a lot of preteaching, which I did during my weekly meetings with them. I included a parent initial column because many parents were curious about what we were doing. This helps make sure parents and homeroom teachers are on the same page, too.

—Jaci Greig (Teacher)

Learning Contract

Name: _____

Date started: _____ **Date due:** _____

Topic: Weather

Standards:

Structural Features of Informational Materials:

- Identify the title, author, illustrator, and table of contents of a reading selection.

Analysis of Grade-Level Appropriate Nonfiction and Informational Text:

- Respond to who, what, when, where, why, and how questions and recognize the main idea of what is read.
- Use context (the meaning of the surrounding text) to understand word and sentence meanings.
- Relate prior knowledge to what is read.

Research Process and Technology:

- Begin asking questions to guide topic selection and ask how and why questions about a topic of interest.
- Identify a variety of sources of information (books, online sources, pictures, charts, tables of contents, diagrams) and document the sources (titles).
- Organize and classify information by constructing categories on the basis of observation.

Goals/Objectives:

- Student will read several nonfiction and fiction books about weather events.
- Student will make connections to existing background knowledge.
- Student will ascertain what conditions cause weather events to occur.
- Student will assess how major weather events can affect people's lives.

Activities:

- Student will be introduced to note-taking strategies and will ascertain the main ideas and details of nonfiction texts.

- Student will create a Venn diagram comparing/contrasting blizzards, hurricanes, and tornadoes.
- Student will use vocabulary word maps to connect to topic vocabulary.
- Student will create a PowerPoint presentation to share how and why major weather events affect our lives.

Resources:
- http://www.stormvideo.com
- *The Magic School Bus: Inside a Hurricane* by Joanna Cole
- *Wild Weather: Blizzards* by Lorraine Jean Hopping
- *Storms* by the Editors of *TIME for Kids*
- *Tornadoes* by Arlene Erlbach
- *The Old Mill* by Margaret Wise Brown
- *The Bears in the Bed and The Great Big Storm* by Paul Bright
- *The Blizzard* by Betty Ren Wright

Product/Outcome:
- Venn diagram
- Vocabulary word maps
- PowerPoint presentation

Evaluation Criteria:
- Student will check in weekly with teacher to monitor progress and receive feedback.
- Rubric will be utilized for the PowerPoint presentation.

Student Signature: _____

Teacher Signature: _____

Parent Signature: _____

Created by Mandy Keele

Real Teacher Comments

This is a learning contract that I used to go along with an independent study project for one of my first graders who is above and beyond the children in my class and is always talking about how she wants to be a meteorologist when she grows up. When I broached the idea of an independent study project with the child and her mother during a parent/teacher conference, they were both very excited. Even though I knew weather held a certain fascination for her, I let her take the lead on what the topic would be. She mentioned several possibilities, but after we discussed it a bit more, she decided that weather would be her topic. She worked on this project during our morning work time (about 10–15 minutes) and then also during our super silent reading time.

—Mandy Keele (Teacher)

Great idea. It is so important for the students to be able to explore areas that are of special interest to them.

—Julia (Colleague)

Developing the learning contract with your student must have been exciting for her and her parents. Creating a PowerPoint to present her findings in first grade is a fabulous learning experience and should stay with her for a long time!

—Jeri (Colleague)

Learning Contract

Student Name: _____

Date Started: _____ **Date Completed:** _____

Grade: Second High Ability

Subject: Language Arts

Topic: Fairy Tales

Standards:
- Student compares and contrasts versions of the same story from different cultures.
- Student writes clear sentences and paragraphs that develop a central idea.
- Student progresses through the stages of the writing process, including prewriting, drafting, revising, and editing multiple drafts.
- Student uses a computer to draft, revise, and publish writing.

Goals and Objectives: Student is able to:
- generate a list of similarities and differences between the two fairy tales;
- create an original Cinderella story;
- evaluate the story for spelling, grammar, and ideas;
- publish the story using the computer; and
- add illustrations that complement the text.

Activities:
- Student will select a nontraditional version of Cinderella to read.
- Student will complete a Venn diagram comparing and contrasting the Cinderella story they read to the traditional Cinderella story read in class.
- Student will write his or her own Cinderella story. Story will contain main characters, setting, plot, and solution.
- Student will publish the story using the computer, including a title page, dedication page, and illustrations.

Resources:
- *The Persian Cinderella* by Shirley Climo
- *Yeh-Shen: A Cinderella Story from China* by Ai-Ling Louie

- *Cinder Edna* by Ellen Jackson
- *Gift of the Crocodile: A Cinderella Story* by Judy Sierra
- *Cindy Ellen: A Wild Western Cinderella* by Susan Lowell
- *Mufaro's Beautiful Daughters: An African Tale* by John Steptoe
- *Cinderella: A Fairy Tale*
- *Baba Yaga and Vasilisa the Brave* by Marianna Mayer

Products:
- Venn diagram
- Published book

Evaluation:
- Weekly conferencing with the teacher to monitor progress and provide feedback
- Rubric will be used for the published Cinderella story

Student Signature: _____

Parent Signature: _____

Teacher Signature: _____

Created by Julia Lester

Real Teacher Comments

This learning contract is for my second-grade high-ability students. These students meet with me once a week for 2 hours. Recently, we started a unit on ancient Egypt. To begin the unit, we read the traditional Cinderella fairy tale and *The Egyptian Cinderella*. Using a Venn diagram, the students compared and contrasted the two stories. Some of the students showed an interest in reading other versions of Cinderella. I designed a learning contract for those students who were interested in reading the different Cinderella stories. They worked on the learning contract during our Challenge period. Each class time, about 20–30 minutes is devoted to working on challenging reading or math packets. Those students who decided to work on the learning contract did this instead of their packets.

—Julia Lester (Teacher)

Even though I teach sixth-grade math, my 3-year-old daughter loves Cinderella, and therefore, I love Cinderella. In all seriousness, I did my student teaching in first grade and can see how well this would work with second graders who have a little higher reading ability. It looks like I am going to be teaching a section of language arts next year, so I am collecting ideas, and I like your ideas here. Now I need to find books appropriate for my level.

—Anthony (Colleague)

Julia, I like that you are capitalizing on students' interests in going above and beyond the curriculum, and I especially like that this is a choice project. That seems like it would really make kids take ownership over the project.

—Lisa (Colleague)

Learning Contract
Topic: Reading

Name: _____

Subject: _____

Date Started: _____ **Date Due:** _____

Standards:
- Student discusses setting, characters, and events in narrative text.
- Student retells up to three events from familiar text using his or her own wording or phrasing.
- Student speaks clearly and audibly in complete, coherent sentences and uses sound effects or illustrations for dramatic effect in narrative and informational presentations.

Goals/Objectives:
- Student will demonstrate his or her story comprehension by reading a book alone, completing an illustration of the story, and orally sharing the sequence of the story events with the class.

Activities:
- Student will select and complete the reading of one book approved by the teacher. The book must be completed within a month.
- Student will illustrate one picture about his or her favorite moment in the book.
- Student will write five sentences explaining what the book is about.
- Student will share his or her book with the class at the end of the month, as well as the illustration.

Resources:
- Student may select one book from the classroom or school library. The book must be at or slightly above the child's reading level and approved by the teacher.

Evaluation Criteria: Student will be graded based on:
- Accuracy and neatness of the illustration.
- Orally providing a correct sequence of events in the story.

Signatures:

Student: _____

Teacher: _____

Parent: _____

Created by Melissa Yekulis

Real Teacher Comments

I've used this learning contract with an advanced kindergarten student who is beyond phonetic recognition needs and is already reading at an advanced level.
—Melissa Yekulis (Teacher)

I really like the activities that you've included for the child to do in the learning contract. The activities appear to be basic enough for me to possibly use with my students who are learning to read in Spanish. Although the age level is different, I feel the learning process for students of both ages in reading would be relatively equivalent. Nicely done!
—Rachel (Colleague)

I agree—this is a good learning contract. I know there is a wide range of readiness/reading levels in a kindergarten class. Your learning contract would help meet the needs of the students who are already readers.
—Sharon (Colleague)

Your activities will help determine the child's comprehension, and the contract will promote independent reading. What a great idea!
—Megan (Colleague)

Learning Contract
Subject: English/Language Arts—Components of a Literary Text

Name: _____

Date Started: _____ **Date Due:** _____

Standards:
- Students read and respond to a wide variety of significant works of children's literature.
- Students are able to analyze grade-level appropriate literary text.
- Students create different endings to stories and identify the problems and the impacts of the different endings.
- Students compare and contrast versions of the same stories from different cultures.
- Students confirm predictions about what will happen next in a story.
- Students recognize the differences between fantasy and reality.
- Students identify the meaning or lesson of a story.
- Students use a computer to draft, revise, and publish writing.
- Students paraphrase information that has been shared orally by others.
- Students organize presentations to maintain a clear focus.
- Students provide descriptions including careful attention to sensory detail.

Objectives:
Students will know:
- The different types of genre.
- The specific literary components that make up a story.
- The many reasons for writing literature.

Students will be able to:
- Describe the character, plot, and setting in stories that they read.
- Categorize a book as being fantasy or reality.
- Paraphrase literary information shared orally.
- Describe the conflict and climax of a book.
- Distinguish if sensory detail is being used in a story to make a story interesting.
- Compare texts to see if changing details impacts the storyline or literary elements.

Activities:
1. Choose two books, one from two different genres:
   - Fantasy
   - Myths/Legends/Fairy Tales
   - Poetry
   - Science Fiction
   - Mystery

Read the two books and describe the plot, characters, and setting of each using either a Microsoft Word document or a PowerPoint presentation. Share this presentation with the class at the end of this learning contract.

2. Choose one book of your choice from the group at the reading center and complete the following:
   - List the title, author, illustrator, and genre category, giving a detailed explanation for the categorization.
   - Describe the conflict and climax of the book, and then create a different ending or climax for the story.

3. Choose one book from the group at the reading center, and complete each step below:
   - Read the book as many times as needed to read it fluently out loud.
   - Use iMovie on the Macintosh computers to video record yourself reading the book. Before reading the story, include the author, illustrator, type of genre, and the literary elements of character, plot, setting, conflict, and climax. While reading the story, emphasize words that add sensory detail to the text.
   - Watch the movie of yourself reading the book and answer these questions:
     - Do I notice when a sentence stops?
     - Does my voice change to show different emotions and to accent sensory detail?
     - Would I enjoy listening to myself reading if I were another student or teacher?

4. Choose one book set (of two books) from the literature sets on the counter. Read both books and compare the literary elements of plot, character, setting, conflict, and climax using an open-ended product.

Possible Books
Poetry:
   Doodle Dandies by J. Patrick Lewis
   Who Swallowed Harold? by Susan Pearson
   A Light in the Attic by Shel Silverstein
   Where the Sidewalk Ends by Shel Silverstein

Mystery:
   A Dark and Noisy Night by Lisa Thiesing
   The Aliens Are Coming! by Lisa Thiesing

Fantasy:
   Mike Fink by Steven Kellogg
   Paul Bunyan by Steven Kellogg
   Pecos Bill by Steven Kellogg

Science Fiction:

June 29, 1999 by David Wiesner

Science Verse by Jon Scieszka

Fairy Tales:

Cinderella; Puss in Boots by Charles Perrault

Cendrillon: A Caribbean Cinderella by Robert D. San Souci

Bigfoot Cinderrrrrella by Tony Johnston

The Korean Cinderella by Shirley Climo

Adelita: A Mexican Cinderella Story by Tomie dePaola

Little Red Riding Hood: A Newfangled Prairie Tale by Lisa Campbell Ernst

Lon Po Po: A Red Riding Hood Story From China by Ed Young

Legends:

The Legend of Sleeping Bear by Kathy-Jo Wargin

The Legend of the Poinsettia by Tomie dePaola

Product/Outcome:

• Students will create an advertisement for the media center to interest other students in a specific genre using the literary elements discussed on this learning contract.

Evaluation Criteria:

• Activities will be used as formative assessments, and students will use feedback from the activities to guide the creation of their products. The products will be used as summative assessment.

Signatures:

Student: _____

Teacher: _____

Parent: _____

Created by Melinda Millholland

Real Teacher Comments

I used this contract with several of with my high-ability second-grade learners. They enjoyed the challenge!

—Melinda Millholland (Teacher)

What a thorough contract! I liked the inclusion of technology and the great selection of literature. I am a bit jealous, too, as my school does not have the technology.

—Jolena (Colleague)

Learning Contract: Solar System

Name: _____

Start Date: _____ Due Date: _____

Standards:
- Locate the title and the name of the author of a book.
- Ask how and why questions about a topic of interest.
- Identify pictures and charts as sources of information and begin gathering information from a variety of sources (books, technology).
- Draw pictures and write words for a specific reason.

Objective:
- Student will gain an understanding of the solar system and learn information about specific planets through the use of nonfiction texts and online sources.

Activities:
- Student will research the solar system and specific planets within the solar system through nonfiction texts and online sources.
- Student will create a book about the planets using the information learned.
- Student will create a representation of the solar system either through a drawing or a model.

Resources:
- *The Planets* by Martha E. H. Rustad
- *The Planets: Neighbours in Space* by Jeanne Bendick
- *The Magic School Bus: Lost in the Solar System* by Joanna Cole
- *Our Solar System* by Seymour Simon
- Others books found in classroom or school library
- http://www.kidsastronomy.com/solar_system.htm
- http://www.kids.nineplanets.org
- http://www.frontiernet.net/~kidpower/astronomy.html

Products:
- Book about planets
- Representation of the solar system

Evaluation:
- Meetings (at least every other day) with the teacher
- Assessment of end products

This contract replaces the regular class work during morning work and calendar time. I understand that I am responsible for working by myself to complete the assignments and that I should use my time wisely and not bother others. I also understand that if I need help or have questions, I may ask the teacher or teaching assistant.

Student Signature: _____

Parent Signature: _____

Teacher Signature: _____

Created by Ashley Peters

Real Teacher Comments

I chose to create a contract for a specific student in my kindergarten class. He is very advanced and has a new fascination with the planets.

—Ashley Peters (Teacher)

Learning Contract

Name: _____

Subject: Science

Date Started: _____ **Date Due:** _____

Standards:

Science
- Understand and demonstrate that everybody can do science.
- Draw pictures and write words to describe objects and experiences.
- Investigate that things move in different ways, such as fast, slowly, etc.

Language Arts
- Understand and follow one- and two-step spoken directions.
- Share information and ideas, speaking in complete, coherent sentences.

Goals/Objectives:

Students will use resources from inside and outside the classroom to create their own simple machines. Students will be able to explain what their simple machines do and how they work.

Topic: Simple machines

Activity:

To complete the contract, you will design and create your own pulley, wheel and axle, lever, wedge, or inclined plane. After you finish your creation, present it to the class and explain what it does and how it works. You will also need to thoroughly explain and/or demonstrate how it makes work easier.

Resources:

- Use the computer to visit the following websites or do research of your own:
  - http://shop.lego.com/Product/?p=9654
  - http://www.henry.k12.ga.us/cur/simp-mach/resources.htm
  - http://atlantis.coe.uh.edu/archive/science/science_lessons/scienceles1/links.htm
  - http://weirdrichard.com/inclined.htm
  - http://sln.fi.edu/qa97/spotlight3/spotlight3.html
  - http://www.mikids.com/Smachines.htm

- Nonfiction books from the library (collected by the teacher)
- Materials found in the classroom or at home (ask permission first)
- Video on simple machines (YouTube)

Evaluation Criteria:

You will be evaluated on what you present to the class and how well you understand simple machines. You will need to explain how your creation works and how it makes work easier.

Signatures:

Student: _____

Teacher: _____

Parent: _____

Created by Kimberly Sapikowski

Real Teacher Comments

I know there are a few students in my classroom who are ready for a learning contract. I believe kindergarten is a tough age to do a learning contract if you're not available to meet with students often or if they don't have parent help; but luckily, I have both. These few students are independent learners who really enjoyed this assignment. I look forward to using learning contracts more as my students and I become more comfortable with them.

—Kimberly Sapikowski (Teacher)

I would imagine that for kindergarteners, learning contracts would work well with only one or two students who were advanced enough to handle it.

—Laura (Colleague)

You know, kindergarteners are at that age where I think I underestimate them. I think I mistakenly still consider them "babies," but I'm constantly surprised at how much they can do. When I plan for my kindergarteners, I always seem to try to water down material. But they can understand much more than I give them credit for. I really like the hands-on activities you offer in your contract. I probably wouldn't ever think to give them these activities, but I'm glad to know they thrived and totally love it!

—Adrienne (Colleague)

I think it is great that you are introducing students to learning contracts at such a young age. Making them aware of their ability to be independent thinkers sets a positive trend. Also, I am sure that it is such a plus to have parental support. I am curious to try this out with a few of my kindergarteners!

—Erin (Colleague)

I am sure that these kids will love the opportunity to take what they've learned and actually create a simple machine. It sounds like you've got the multitasking aspect covered with some parent help, if needed. Great idea!

—Mandy (Colleague)

Your learning contract on simple machines is great! I might have to steal your idea if you don't care. I completely agree that at the kindergarten level, the kids are going to need more support, especially in the beginning. I think that as they become more familiar with the process, they will be able to be more independent. I guess there has to be a starting point somewhere, and for some students, it would be completely appropriate to begin this in kindergarten.

—Ashley (Colleague)

Learning Contract

Name: _____

Subject: Math

Date Started: _____ **Date Due:** _____

Goals/Objectives:
Student will:
- Understand the values of pennies, nickels, dimes, and quarters.
- Calculate the sum of two items purchased with coins.
- Evaluate if coins used to purchase products are correct.
- Determine the amount of change due to a "customer."
- Count back the change with the appropriate coins.

Topic: Money and problem solving

Activities:
Student will set up a student store in the classroom as a center for students to visit during math group time. Student will place price tags on the products and serve as the cashier using plastic coins.

Resources:
- Student will need to get boxes and containers to use for the store as products. (These can be either from the student's home or requested of the class or staff members in the form of a letter.)
- Students will use plastic coins from the classroom. Paper will be provided for price tags and receipts. Coin stampers and inkpads from the classroom may also be used on the receipts to show which coins were used to pay and/or give change.

Product/Outcome:
The intended outcome is for the student to set up a store to be used as a center in class during math groups for 3 days to allow all of the other students to "shop." The student will demonstrate mastery of the goals by providing items for the store, calculating the amount needed to buy items, and counting out the correct coins for change.

Evaluation Criteria:
Detailed receipts will be collected showing the items purchased, the price for each item, the total amount for all items, the amount paid, the amount returned, and which coins were used. A rubric will be used to evaluate the store, to evaluate the student's performance as a cashier, and to evaluate the accuracy of the receipts.

Signatures:

Student: _____

Teacher: _____

Parent: _____

Rubric for Money Math Learning Contract

Store Items

0 points	5 points	10 points	15 points
Did not bring in boxes or containers for the student store	Brought in only 2 or 3 items for the student store	Brought in 4–7 items for the student store	Brought in at least 8 items for the student store

Price Tags and Receipts

0 points	5 points	10 points	15 points
Did not provide price tags and/or receipts	Provided tags or receipts, but not both	Provided tags and receipts	Provided tags and receipts with attention to detail

Receipt Accuracy

0 points	5 points	10 points	15 points
Receipts had a 69% or lower accuracy rate	Receipts had a 70%–79% accuracy rate	Receipts had an 80%–89% accuracy rate	Receipts had a 90%–100% accuracy rate

Cashiering Skills

0 points	5 points	10 points	15 points
Did not allow many students to participate; was not courteous in manner or helpful	Was somewhat helpful; allowed some students a chance to participate	Allowed most students to participate; helped many; was mostly courteous	Allowed for maximum student participation; aided all students in counting money (if needed); acted in a courteous manner

Name: _____ **Total Points earned:** _____/60

Created by Shannon Anderson

Real Teacher Comments

I decided to do my learning contract on counting money. The student did this in place of the two chapters on money in the first-grade math series after she had pretested out of that material.

—Shannon Anderson (Teacher)

I like the idea of letting the student have a store. I'm sure everyone in your class enjoyed it. I also like that you added your rubric to your contract.

—Brenda (Colleague)

I LOVE the idea of the store! You could tie that into an incentive plan for your classroom. Plus, the skills are real-life.

—Sharon (Colleague)

Setting up a store looks like a really fun way to help with this lesson.

—Jason (Colleague)

Wow! What a great real-life connection!

—Megan (Colleague)

Learning Contract

Name: _____

Subject: Math

Beginning Date: _____ **Check-In Date:** _____

Due Date: _____

This contract replaces the regular class work for money.

During math, I will need to complete the activities listed below in the order in which they are written. When I am finished, I will participate in a discussion with the teacher.

1. _____ Review how to count quarters, dimes, nickels, and pennies by playing the counting money game on this website: http://fen.com/studentactivities/Piggybank/piggybank.html. Keep playing until you can fill up the piggy bank.

2. _____ There are many ways to make $1.00. How many ways can you use the quarters, dimes, nickels, and pennies to make $1.00? Draw your answers on the answer sheet.

3. _____ Go shopping in the newspaper ads. Choose two items you would like to buy. Cut them out and glue them to your paper. Find the cost of the two items together. Use the money stamps to show how you would pay for the items.

4. _____ Sometimes customers don't have exact change to pay for goods. They need to get change back from the cashier. Choose at least 10 items from the picture cards to buy. Pretend you only have bills to pay the cashier. Show the coins you will get back with the money stamps. Use the real money to check your answers.

I realize I must work independently during math and not interrupt others. I must use my time and resources wisely.

Student Signature: _____

Teacher Signature: _____

Parent Signature: _____

This learning contract is targeted at students who have already mastered the first-grade concept of understanding the values of pennies, nickels, and dimes, and who can masterfully count collections of pennies, nickels, and dimes. The included activities push their learning and practice in authentic situations.

Mathematics Standards:

- Identify and give the values of collections of pennies, nickels, and dimes.
- Choose the approach, materials, and strategies used in solving problems.
- Use tools such as objects or drawings to model problems.
- Make precise calculations and check the validity of the results in the context of the problem.

Resources Needed:

- Computer with Internet access
- Money stamps and stamp pad or plastic quarters, dimes, nickels, and pennies
- Shopping ads from local newspaper
- Pencils, scissors, and glue sticks

Products: Activities 2, 3, and 4 will have written products.

Assessment: Products will be checked for completeness and accuracy.

Created by Kristen Shively

Real Teacher Comments

I created a learning contract for my kindergarten students who have already mastered counting pennies, nickels, and dimes (a first-grade standard). I have some students who can also count quarters, so I tried to make the activities more complicated and speed up the pacing by including activities with quarters and dollars. I also tried to incorporate higher level addition and subtraction skills.

—Kristen Shively (Teacher)

I think it would be so much fun to be in your class. I liked the variety of activities that are definitely kid-friendly. I especially liked the shopping and making change activities. I think this will be a useful contract for years to come. Nice work.

—Dawn (Colleague)

My first graders are working on money counting skills as well. I loved your ideas!

—Erica (Colleague)

CHAPTER 7
TIERED LESSONS

Overview

According to Adams and Pierce (2006), tiered lessons are designed for all students to address the same academic standard or concept, but at varying levels of depth, complexity, or structure. Tomlinson (1999) indicated that tiered lessons are staples for differented instruction. Tiered lessons allow several pathways for students to arrive at an essential understanding based on the students' readiness. Erickson (2002) described essential understanding as "the key principles and generalizations that develop from the fact base . . . They are the 'big ideas' that transfer through time and across cultures" (p. 47). Implementing a tiered lesson implies that the teacher has a good understanding of the students' ability levels with respect to the lesson and has developed the tiers to meet those needs. The number of tiers depends on the range of ability levels in the classroom.

How and When to Use Tiered Lessons

Use tiered lessons any time you need students to work on similar material but at varying levels of readiness. For example, readiness can be reflected in skill level, reading level, and ability to handle multiple sets of directions. As we noted before (Adams & Pierce, 2006), many examples of tiered lessons have three tiers: below grade level, at grade level, and above grade level. There is no rule that states there may be only three tiers, however. The number of tiers depends on the range of ability levels in the classroom. Remember: You will be forming tiers based on the assessment of your students' abilities to handle the material particular to the lesson. Students are regrouped when you decide to move to a different lesson. The number of groups per tier will vary, as will the number of students per tier. Do not try to form groups of equal size; instead, groups should be formed based on the readiness needs of individual students. For example, Tier I may have two groups of three students; Tier II may have five groups of four students; and Tier III may have one group of two students. Even if students are already grouped into classes by ability, there is still variability at each ability level, and teachers still need to address these varied ability levels in each population. What you don't want is for students' tiers to differ in the *amount* of work they have to do, rather than the *kind* of work they do. Second, be sure that each tier is doing moderately challenging and developmentally appropriate work. In other words, no group should be given busy work. One group should not be doing "black line" practice sheets while another does a fabulous experiment.

Directions for Making Tiered Lessons

According to Adams and Pierce (2006), there are nine steps to developing a tiered lesson.

1. Identify the grade level and subject for which you will write the lesson.
2. Identify the standard (e.g., national, state, and/or local) that you are targeting. A common mistake for those just beginning to tier is to develop three great activities and then try to force them into a tiered lesson. Start with the standard first. If you don't know where you are going, how will you know if you get there?
3. Identify the key concept and essential understanding. The key concept follows from the standard. Ask yourself, "What 'Big Idea' am I targeting?" The essential understanding follows from the concept. Ask yourself, "What do I want the students to know at the end of the lesson, regardless of their placement in the tiers?"
4. Develop a powerful lesson that addresses the essential understanding. This will be the base from which you develop your tiers.
5. Identify the background information necessary to complete the lesson, and be sure that students have this information, so that they can be successful in the lesson. What scaffolding is necessary? What must you already have covered, or what must the student already have learned? Are there other skills that must be taught first?
6. Determine which element of the lesson you will tier. You may choose to tier the content (what you want the students to learn), the process (the way students make sense out of the content), or the product (the outcome at the end of a lesson, lesson set, or unit—often a project).
7. Determine the readiness of your students. Readiness is based on the ability levels of the students. Preassessment is a good method of determining readiness.

8. Determine how many tiers you will need, using your assessment of the students' readiness to engage in the lesson based on its focus.

9. Determine the appropriate assessment(s) you will use based on your activities. Both formative and summative assessments may be included in the lesson (pp. 21–22).

How the Strategy Fits in the CIRCLE MAP

Tiered lessons fit in the "differentiated instructional strategies" component of the CIRCLE MAP as a whole-group activity. Tiered lessons accommodate a variety of readiness levels through whole-class instruction: All students work with the same standard and concept, but they follow different pathways leading toward the same essential understanding.

Examples

The examples we have chosen include lessons for specific topics and grade levels that may be readily adapted to other grade levels. These lessons were created by real teachers who have used them in their own classrooms. When possible, we have included comments from these teachers and their colleagues with the intention that their comments may provide additional insight into developing your own tiered lessons.

For example, Mike Johnson's first-grade science class is studying plants. They have studied the parts of a plant and have identified differences between plants and animals. They are now ready to design an investigation of the factors that influence the growth of plants. Mr. Johnson always provides opportunities for hands-on investigation in his class and believes in allowing the students to work like scientists. Based on his assessment of his students' ability to design a scientific investigation, he divides his class into three tiers. Each tier will be designing an experiment about plant growth, hypothesizing, controlling variables, gathering and analyzing data, and drawing conclusions. Each tier will use the same materials and work on designing an investigation into what makes plants grow. The difference between the tiers is the amount of scaffolding Mr. Johnson provides. For example, the students who need the most assistance with the experiment receive a sheet with prompts that guide them through the process, while those students who have more advanced skills are designing their own experiment and will check their designs with Mr. Johnson before starting. To allow maximum student participation, Mr. Johnson divides the students in each tier into groups of three or four. While students are working on their experiments, Mr. Johnson rotates from group to group to observe student progress.

Template

Title of Tiered Lesson

Subject:

Grade:

Standard(s):

Key Concept:

Essential Understanding:

Background:

Tiered in Content, Process, or Product (choose one)

Tier I:

Tier II:

Tier III:

Assessment:

Tiered Lesson

Subject: Math/Measurement

Grade: First

Standard: Measure the length of an object to the nearest inch or centimeter.

Key Concept: Measurement

Essential Understanding: Measuring an object helps us find out something about the object.

Background:
Before beginning this lesson, students should know how to properly measure items using standard measurement tools. They should understand the placement and movement of a measuring tool.

Tiered in Process

Tiered According to Readiness
Students will be given a group of items to measure. Items could include small toys, paper, books, cardboard boxes, blocks, pencils, and other items readily found in the classroom. Students will be given rulers, yardsticks, meter sticks, trundle wheels, and tape measures.

Tier I:
Directions: Select three objects from those provided and measure them in some way. On the paper provided, draw a picture of the object and write a measurement sentence that describes the object. Be sure to include what you used to measure the object.

Example: I used a ruler to measure the pencil (picture). It was 7 inches long.

Tier II:
Directions: Select three objects from those provided and measure them. Your challenge is to measure the object in as many different ways as possible.

Example: The chair is 3 feet tall. It is 16 inches wide. Each leg is 2 inches wide.

Tier III:
Directions: Select one object from those provided. How many different ways can you describe the same measurement of that object? Draw a picture of the object and write two measurement sentences that describe the same characteristic of that object.

Example: The chair is 3 feet tall. It is 36 inches tall. It is about one meter tall. It is one yard tall.

Complete this activity for several different items.

Assessment:
This is a formative assessment activity. This activity provides time for "kid watching." Teacher observation can take place while the students are measuring. Based on these observations, the teacher can readily assess who has mastered this concept and who is still struggling.

Created by Sharon Boggs

Real Teacher Comments

My students love to work on hands-on projects. By having them measure different objects, this activity gets them to think creatively about the different ways to measure them, as well as to work on the actual skills of measuring them. It helps to put them in groups, because they can work with each other and compare answers to get better in areas where they're having difficulty.

—Sharon Boggs (Teacher)

I feel like you'll definitely want to show the Tier III group an example; it sounds confusing at first. But I think they love looking for things to measure around the room.

—Megan (Colleague)

Tiered Learning

Subject: Reading

Grade: First

Standards:
Standard 1: Work Recognition, Fluency, and Vocabulary Development
Standard 2: Comprehension of Nonfiction
Standard 3: Comprehension and Analysis of Literary Text

Key Concept: Comprehension

Essential Understanding: Good readers use different strategies when they read to help them understand what they are reading.

Background:
The students in this classroom have reading levels ranging from emergent readers to fluent readers. Their reading level grade equivalencies range from kindergarten to fourth grade. Reading lessons and practice must be differentiated in order to meet the learning needs of all students.

Tiered in Content

Tiered According to Readiness

Students in all tiers will be given texts that are at the appropriate level for their current reading readiness. Trade books and picture books will be used for reading material. Students not meeting with the teacher will read independently from books chosen to fit their reading level and their interests.

Tier I: Emergent Readers
Students in this tier will meet with the teacher daily in small groups to learn and practice reading strategies for decoding and for comprehension. A heavier emphasis will be placed on decoding strategies for this group. They will also meet with the teacher individually twice per week for ongoing assessment.

Tier II: Transitional Readers
Students in this group will meet with the teacher three times per week in small groups to learn and practice reading strategies. Although decoding strategies will be utilized, a heavier emphasis will be on comprehension strategies. These students will also meet with the teacher individually twice per week for ongoing assessment.

Tier III: Fluent Readers
Students in this group are reading fluently above grade level. They will meet with the teacher one or two times per week for literature discussion, comprehension strategy lessons, and to practice oral fluency. These students will meet with the teacher individually once per week for ongoing assessment.

Assessment:
Assessment will include the following:
Retelling Rubric—to assess comprehension
Literature Response Sheets—to assess comprehension
Running Records—to assess oral reading/decoding

Created by Rhonda Brandt

Real Teacher Comments

This is basically how my reading workshop works every day in my classroom. I have used Developmental Reading Assessments (DRAs) and the STAR Reading assessments, along with my ongoing assessments to match readers to trade books at their level. They choose books at their level that interest them. While I meet with small groups and conference with students individually, other students read independently. The first several weeks of school, we spend a great deal of time on how to work independently and practicing. Our work time rules are "Ask 3 Before Me," "Use a 6-inch Voice," and "Work the Whole Time." Sometimes students are also asked to complete reading responses or to work with partners.

—Rhonda Brandt (Teacher)

You are right on target about needing to teach them how to work independently. Otherwise, you get chaos. I use the "Ask 3" rule and the "6-Inch voice rule." I couldn't do without those!

—Sam (Colleague)

Tiered Learning

Subject: Social Studies

Grade: Second

Standard: Identify real people and fictional characters who were good leaders and good citizens, and explain the qualities that make them admirable, such as honesty and trustworthiness.

Key Concept: Leadership/Citizenship

Essential Understanding: Good leaders and good citizens have similar characteristics or qualities.

Background:
The qualities of a good citizen have been introduced and discussed.

Available materials should include: copies of the books for each group, paper to list the qualities of each character, pencils, a blank Venn diagram on chart paper for each group, and markers. The students are placed in groups according to reading levels.

Tiered in Content

Tiered According to Readiness

Tier I: Struggling Learners (May need material read aloud or use listening stations)
Students will read *Helen Keller* by Sean Dolan on Day 1 and *The Three Little Pigs* by Margaret Hillert on Day 2.

Tier II: At Grade Level Learners
Students will read *Abraham Lincoln* by Wil Mara on Day 1 and *Korka the Mighty Elf* by Linda Strachan on Day 2.

Tier III: Advanced Learners
Students will read *Martin Luther King Jr.* by Lola M. Schaefer on Day 1 and *Save the River* by Sarah Glasscock on Day 2.

Assessment:
Day 1: Students will work as a group to create a list of qualities of the main character that makes him or her a good leader. They will create a separate list of qualities demonstrating good citizenship. They will then highlight the characteristics that overlap in each list. Finally, the group will create a Venn diagram on chart paper to compare and contrast the characteristics of good leaders and good citizens.

Day 2: After reading the book, students will compare the fictional main character from Day 2 to the real-life character from Day 1. They will make a list of the qualities that the characters share and especially of any new qualities that they found in the fictional character. They will then add to their Venn diagrams by using Post-It® Notes to add new qualities of the fictional character and a highlighter to highlight qualities that the two characters share.

Created by Molly Davis

Real Teacher Comments

We make a whole unit out of being good neighbors and citizens. My students enjoy the hands-on activities. It really keeps them engaged and helps them remember the details of the lesson easier. We practiced working independently at the beginning of the year, so my students work well when they are grouped and doing different things.

—Molly Davis (Teacher)

Great idea incorporating a Venn diagram! I know my students would love being able to use a highlighter and Post-Its® to learn as well.

—Lauren (Colleague)

Tiered Learning

Subject: Math

Grade: Second grade

Standards:
- Construct squares, rectangles, triangles, cubes, and rectangular prisms with appropriate materials.
- Describe, classify, and sort plane and solid geometric shapes (triangle, square, rectangle, cube, rectangular prism) according to the number and shape of faces, and the number of edges and vertices.
- Recognize geometric shapes and structures in the environment and specify their locations.

Key Concept: Shapes

Essential Understanding: Plane and solid figures have edges, vertices, and angles that make them identifiable.

Background:
Plane and solid shapes have been introduced in class. Students have learned the names of each of the shapes and have had the opportunity to manipulate two- and three-dimensional shapes.

Tiered in Product

Tiered According to Readiness

Tier I:
This activity is for students who are still having difficulty with the shapes and solids. Students are given two large hula hoops and an assortment of objects that contain plane shapes or are a solid shape. The students are asked to create three different Venn diagrams with the objects. Students must name each part of the Venn diagram. After each Venn diagram is created with the hula hoops, the students need to either write or draw the Venn diagram on chart paper.

Tier II:
These students have a good understanding of shapes and solids. Students are given an assortment of objects that contain plane shapes or are a solid shape. The students have a large sheet of chart paper that is divided into four sections. Section 1 is titled: "5 Shapes With a Total of 20 or More Faces." Section 2 is titled: "Two by Two Group" In this group the students need to find a plane and solid shape that share characteristics (e.g., a basketball and a round magnet). Section 3 is titled: "Build and Name Me." The

students need to use five different shapes to create an alien and have to give their new alien a name. Section 4 is titled: "What Else." In this section, the students are encouraged to draw four things that could be found in the classroom that fit into a particular group such as "the sphere group" or the "6 faces, 12 edges, and 8 vertices group." They will need to identify the group with a name. Students will work together on this project.

Tier III:
These students have mastered the standards dealing with shapes and solids at second-grade level. In this activity, the students are introduced to other three-dimensional shapes that are not covered in the second-grade curriculum. They will receive paper patterns and will be asked to build the shape from the pattern with a partner. After completing the shape, the student will count up faces, edges, and vertices. Then, the group will get together and compare shapes and create a table with the name of the shape as well as its attributes in order from greatest to least. Finally, the group will brainstorm where they might have seen these shapes in their environment.

Anchoring Activities:
1. Pattern blocks and pattern block cards where students create things such as clown faces or sailboats.
2. Pattern blocks and blank pieces of paper. Directions: Design something with pattern blocks. Then write a creative story about your design.

Assessment:
For each tier the teacher will look at the end product and determine if the groups understand the concepts. The tiered lesson products will be used to determine understanding of material and will be the basis for additional lessons.

Created by Vicki Heil

Real Teacher Comments

I decided to do a tiered math lesson covering our current topic of shapes. Because I differentiate my math lessons already, my students are used to flexible grouping depending on their level of understanding of the concepts. I have a rather large classroom, and I use tables instead of desks, which makes it very easy to push things out of our way and work on the floor. My room easily handles three groups of students doing three different activities, and the students are far enough away from each other that they seldom worry about what the other group is doing until the end of the lesson.

Tiers I and II went pretty smoothly, and I was able to move in and out of the groups rather easily and gave very little prompting. Tier III was a little more difficult. The patterns were a little tough for them to put together; however, they really enjoy learning some other geometric shapes.

—Vicki Heil (Teacher)

I try to remember to make sure that all groups have equally engaging tasks, and you seemed to do that. From the hula-hoops, to the aliens, to making real-world connections, it seemed that all the students would enjoy their specific tasks. I like your anchor activities, which are necessary because you never know exactly how long it will take a group to complete their task.

—Daniel (Colleague)

I really like the hula-hoop idea—that's a great hands-on way to do Venn diagrams!

—Kimberly (Colleague)

I love the hula-hoop idea—so obvious, yet I never thought about it. They could be used in almost any curriculum as well. I can't wait to use them in my classroom.

—Erin (Colleague)

I found it very interesting that your high group was the group that needed you the most. This is probably not what most people would expect. It just goes to show that just because kids are high ability doesn't mean they don't need the support and guidance of a teacher.

—Ashley (Colleague)

Tiered Learning

Subject: Language Arts

Grade: First

Standard: Correctly write complete sentences.

Key Concept: Structure

Essential Understanding: Sentences need a subject and a predicate in order to be complete.

Background:
Students have recently been introduced to the terms *subject* and *predicate*. We have discussed that sentences contain complete thoughts; however, in their writing, they have a tendency to often write either fragments or the "never-ending" run-on sentences. By introducing them to these concepts, I hope to increase their awareness of what elements are needed for a complete sentence and when to punctuate.

Tiered in Process

Tiered According to Readiness

Tier I:
This tier is for my struggling writers. There are cards with subjects and cards with predicates, but they are not labeled as such. The students will match up a subject and a predicate to create a complete sentence. They will then label the parts with an S for subject or a P for predicate.

Tier II:
This tier is for those children who tend to write in run-on sentences and don't yet fully understand where they need to place that period. The students will work with partially completed sentence strips. The strip will contain either a subject or a predicate. The students will add either a missing subject or predicate, label the parts with an S or a P, and add the ending punctuation.

Tier III:
This is for children who generally write in complete sentences. For this activity, they will write their own sentences but are asked to color code them. They should write their subjects in one color and their predicates in another color.

Assessment:

As children work on these activities, the teacher will observe and, afterwards, will use the exit card below to determine follow-up instruction.

Sentence Exit Card

Please circle what is missing.

The groundhog.	Subject	Predicate
Hopped over the wooden fence.	Subject	Predicate
Gives me a cupcake.	Subject	Predicate

Write 2 complete sentences. Please circle the subject and underline the predicate.

_____

_____

_____

_____

Created by Mandy Keele

Real Teacher Comments

I've recently introduced my students to the terms subject and predicate in hopes of creating a connection to the mechanics involved in writing a complete sentence and where a period goes. Several of them have a tendency not to punctuate. I talked about how, even in our writing, we can see patterns. Sentence: subject, predicate, period. Next sentence: subject, predicate, period, and so on. We talked about the subject's role versus the predicate's role. We used the following website to identify whether the highlighted section of the sentence was the subject, predicate, or neither: http://www.myschoolhouse.com/courses/O/1/55.asp.

I then gave every child a card with either a subject or a predicate on it. Subjects went to one side of the room, and predicates to the other. Then, a "subject" and a "predicate" would meet in the middle of the room to combine themselves into a complete sentence. I was holding the big piece of paper with a period on it. Of course, the sentences they created were often silly (which they loved).

After that warm-up activity, they broke into their groups for the tiered lesson. As expected, my Tier I group needed a little more support. There were a couple of children in Tier II who picked up on it so quickly that they probably could have handled being in Tier III, which had fewer supports in place. I also loved using the exit card as a quick assessment.

—Mandy Keele (Teacher)

I like the inclusion of the exit card. You just inspired me to create some exit cards to include at the end of our weekly spelling tests for the remainder of the year. I have been looking for a simple way to assess the effectiveness of our grammar mini-lessons, and this could be it!

—Jason (Colleague)

I liked your idea of giving the students cards with subjects and predicates on them. I teach the first grade high literacy group, and one day a week during literacy, we focus on writing. Although these students have been identified as high readers, some of them struggle to make complete sentences. This would be a great way for me to help them make their wonderful ideas into compete sentences.

—Julia (Colleague)

I can only imagine the excitement in your room when you did the hands-on activity where the kids combined to make a complete sentence. What a great way to get the kids excited about the topic! I also love the exit card. It was a great way to gather important information about what your students knew without taking up a lot of time.

—Ashley (Colleague)

Tiered Learning

Subject: Math

Grade: First

Standard: The learner will be able to use a calendar to identify specific dates and to differentiate between a week and a day.

Key Concept: Time

Essential Understanding: A calendar helps us keep track of time such as days, months, and years.

Background:
Students are used to working on calendar skills on a daily basis. Students know the days of the week.

Tiered in Content

Tiered According to Readiness

Tier I:
Give the students a copy of a completed calendar (e.g., March). Have the students copy the calendar on a blank calendar page. Using their completed calendar, students will answer questions about the calendar. Teacher may need to help in reading the questions. Some sample questions are:

What day of the week is the 10th on?

How many Mondays are in this month?

How many days are in this month?

What is the name of this month?

What day of the week is the 22nd on?

How many days are in one week?

How many days do we go to school in a week?

Tier II:

Using a calendar that is not completed (has missing numbers), the students will complete the calendar. After completing the calendar, they will answer questions such as:

What day of the week is the 10th on?

How many Tuesdays are in this month?

How many days are in this month?

How many days would we go to school in this month?

What day of the week does this month begin on?

What would be the next month?

Are there more Tuesdays than Saturdays? If so, how many more?

Tier III:

Students will be given a completed calendar (e.g., March) and a blank calendar. Students are to make a calendar of the month after the completed calendar (e.g., April). Students will then answer questions about the new calendar:

How many days does your calendar have?

What month is your calendar?

How many Saturdays are in the month?

How many days would you go to school in that month?

On what day of the week did your calendar begin?

Compare the two calendars and write two differences.

Assessment:

Document if the students are able to read a calendar and answer questions about the calendar. Determine if the students were able to copy, complete, or make the calendar correctly. Observe the students while they are working to determine if they are able to properly answer the questions in their groups.

Created by Loree Marroquin

Real Teacher Comments

Every morning I have circle time with my students. Here we discuss the weather and add the new day to the wall calendar. We also practice our days of the week, and the students now know them. However, it was important that the students learn about the calendar in ways other than just repeating the sayings and songs we give them. This lesson really has them think and work on honing those skills.

—Loree Marroquin (Teacher)

It could also be neat to work with holidays with some of your advanced groups. For example, on which day of the week is St. Patrick's Day (if using a March calendar)?

—Daniel (Colleague)

I love that while this is incorporated into math (e.g., numbers, days), you can also adapt it into other subjects like science (What is weather usually like in this month?) and social studies (What holidays happen in the month of December?).

—Jeri (Colleague)

Tiered Learning

Subject: Math

Grade: Kindergarten

Standards:
- Compare sets of up to 10 objects and identify whether one set is equal to, more than, or less than another.
- Divide sets of 10 or fewer objects into equal parts.
- Record and organize information using objects and pictures.

Key Concept: Division

Essential Understanding: Students will illustrate their knowledge of equal groups by dividing a number of objects into equal groups using pictures to represent their information.

Background:
The students have been introduced to the topic of distributing an amount equally among a given number of groups through a few class discussions with examples completed together as a whole group. The students have also completed sets of problems individually and then shared their answers as a class and discussed them further. The students have been taught to use pictures to help them represent their information and complete their work. Materials will be made available for those students in need of more assistance, including large circle cut-outs, cubes, rods, and counters.

Tiered in Content

Tiered According to Readiness

Tier I:
This tier is designed for the students not yet working at grade level. Using pictures or objects, students will demonstrate how to equally distribute six items among three circles. Students will repeat the procedure with nine items. Each student will work individually to solve the problems given to them.

Tier II:
This tier is designed for the students working at grade level. Using pictures or objects, students will demonstrate how to equally distribute 12, 14, or 15 items among two or three circles. Students may choose which of these numbers to use. Each student will work individually using pictures or with manipulatives (if needed) to solve the problems given to them.

Tier III:

This tier is designed for the students working above grade level. Students have three, four, and five circles and will evenly distribute the given number of items among their circles. They will need to determine which circle to use for equal distribution. Students should be encouraged to try multiple solutions. Each student will work individually with manipulatives (if needed) to solve the problems given to them. After completing the first two problems, the student will also be asked to use their higher order thinking skills to solve a more difficult problem.

Assessment:

After the students have completed their activities, the teacher will use a summative assessment to determine the students' abilities to divide sums into equal groups and to recognize and check to see if they divided them among the groups equally. The teacher will make notes on the students' charts answering the following question: Could the student explain how to divide up the large number into equal groups and how he or she knows the groups have an equal number of items in each of them? For Tier III, students will be asked how they approached the third problem.

Making Sense of Equal Groups
Tier 1

Name _____

1. Divide 6 equally among the 2. Be sure to check your work.
2. Divide 9 equally among the 3. Be sure to check your work.

Making Sense of Equal Groups
Tier 2

Name _____

1. Divide 12 equally among the 3. Be sure to check your work.
2. Divide 15 equally among the 3. Be sure to check your work.

Making Sense of Equal Groups
Tier 3

Name _____

1. Divide 20 chocolate chips equally. Figure out if you need three, four, or five cookies. Is there more than one answer?

2. Divide 15 pepperonis equally. Figure out if you need three, four, or five pizzas. Is there more than one answer?

3. Can you figure out how many pieces of candy you would need if you wanted to be able to distribute them equally so it didn't matter if you had 3, 4, or 5 trick-or-treat bags?

Created by Kimberly Sapikowski

Real Teacher Comments

My Tiered Lesson was geared toward kindergarten math. I designed it for the section we just recently learned—dividing large sums into equal groups. Because I have already seen what the students know about the topic, I had a good idea of which tier to place them in based on readiness, and I ended up with three groups—those currently working below grade level, those at grade level, and those above grade level. Before distributing the assignment, I explained the directions to the students and also explained that not everyone's assignment would look the same. Because I put the assignment in partially written form, and knowing that some of them would not be able to read it, I also explained they could ask me questions about reading the problem, but that I would not be answering any questions about the math part itself. I walked around while the students worked to see how particular students were doing and to answer questions, but I mainly took notes at the end, as I used this as a summative assessment.

Most of the students zipped right through the page without much hesitation—a good sign—and a few took some time to complete it. In looking through the sheets, I had a few surprises in both directions—one student whom I am usually helping complete every assignment did it quickly, without any help, and did it right! I am sure I will look at putting that student in the second/middle tier for the next time around, as she was in the first/low one and did very well. On the flipside, one of the students who I put in the highest tier did not do very well on this particular assignment, and I will be speaking with that student to see where the struggle might have been. I will reassess for the next activity.

—Kimberly Sapikowski (Teacher)

I really like how you took the time to evaluate if you had the students in the correct tiers. Even the student you thought would do really well kind of surprised you. I appreciate that you didn't just brush that off and that you are planning on doing something about it. It seems like the most effective tiering contains constant evaluation to see if the kids are at the right level.

—Adrienne (Colleague)

It does seem that you have to constantly assess and reassess, which is why I believe flexible grouping is stressed when differentiating. Your kids are constantly growing and changing, so you have got to keep on it.

—Kimberly (Teacher)

REFERENCES

Adams, C. M., & Pierce, R. L. (2006). *Differentiating instruction: A practical guide to tiering lessons in the elementary grades.* Waco, TX: Prufrock Press.

Coil, C. (2007). *Successful teaching in the differentiated classroom.* Marion, IL: Pieces of Learning.

Erickson, H. L. (2002). *Concept-based curriculum and instruction.* Thousand Oaks, CA: Corwin Press.

Gregory, G. H., & Chapman, C. (2002). *Differentiated instructional strategies: One size doesn't fit all.* Thousand Oaks, CA: Corwin Press.

Kingore, B. (2004). *Differentiation: Simplified, realistic, and effective: How to challenge advanced potentials in mixed-ability classrooms.* Austin, TX: Professional Associates.

Passow, A. H. (1982). *Differentiated curricula for the gifted/talented: A point of view.* Ventura, CA: Ventura County Superintendent of Schools Office.

Tomlinson, C. A. (1999). *The differentiated classroom: Responding to the needs of all learners.* Alexandria, VA: ASCD.

Tomlinson, C. A. (2001). *How to differentiate instruction in mixed-ability classrooms* (2nd ed.). Alexandria, VA: ASCD.

Tomlinson, C. A. (2003). *Fulfilling the promise of the differentiated classroom.* Alexandria, VA: ASCD.

Ward, V. (1980). *Differential education for the gifted.* Ventura, CA: National/State Leadership Training Institute for the Gifted and Talented.

Winebrenner, S. A. (1992). *Teaching gifted kids in the regular classroom: Strategies and techniques every teacher can use to meet the academic needs of the gifted and talented.* Minneapolis, MN: Free Spirit.

ABOUT THE AUTHORS

Cheryll M. Adams is the director of the Center for Gifted Studies and Talent Development at Ball State University. She teaches graduate courses for the license in gifted education. For the past 30 years, she has served in the field of gifted education as a teacher of gifted students at all grade levels, Director of Academic Life at the Indiana Academy for Science, Mathematics, and Humanities, and as the principal teacher in the Ball State Institute for the Gifted in Mathematics program. Additionally, she has been the founder and director of various other programs for gifted students. Dr. Adams has authored or coauthored numerous publications in professional journals, as well as several book chapters. She serves on the editorial review board for *Roeper Review, Gifted Child Quarterly, Journal for the Education of the Gifted*, and *The Teacher Educator*. She has served on the Board of Directors of the National Association for Gifted Children, has been president of the Indiana Association for the Gifted, and currently serves on the board of The Association for the Gifted, Council for Exceptional Children. In 2002 she received the NAGC Early Leader Award.

Rebecca L. Pierce is associate professor of mathematical sciences at Ball State University and fellow at the Center for Gifted Studies and Talent Development. She teaches undergraduate and graduate courses in mathematics and statistics. For the last 35 years, Dr. Pierce has taught mathematics to elementary, middle school, high school, and college students. Dr. Pierce directs the Ball State Institute for the Gifted in Mathematics. Additionally, she worked as a Senior Research Engineer for Bell Helicopter and as a statistical consultant for a variety of industries. She has authored or coauthored numerous publications in professional journals, as well as several book chapters. She is the chair of Mathematics Day, a program for middle school girls interested in mathematics. She serves as a reviewer for *Roeper Review, Gifted Child Quarterly, Journal for the Education of the Gifted*, and *The Teacher*

Educator. She received the Leadership Award from the Indiana Association for the Gifted in 2002.

Dr. Adams and Dr. Pierce work with teachers throughout the United States and Europe toward establishing more effectively differentiated classrooms through the use of the CIRCLE MAP. In addition, they provide professional development and consultation in the areas of mathematics, science, identification, and program evaluation. They have coauthored and received three Javits grants from the federal government in partnership with the Indiana schools.